BRUISES

DIVORCE   CRAZYLAND   JIU-JITSU

BRUISES

A Memoir by
Michael R. Simpson

STORY MERCHANT BOOKS
BEVERLY HILLS
2013

Story Merchant Books
9601 Wilshire Boulevard #1202
Beverly Hills CA 90210
http://www.storymerchant.com/books.html

Ilustrations: Joy Skaw
Editor: Lisa Cerasoli
Cover and book design: www.aulicinodesign.com

Acknowledgements

My inspiration for this book is not complicated; every boy wants to be a super hero and every man thinks he is one until something devastating happens that forces him to recreate himself or he perishes. I also have a love of good quotes and have used them as my inner guide when reason was out to lunch or happy hour. Most importantly, jiu-jitsu has changed my life. This book is a Venn diagram of these three universes. I hope it's an enjoyable read that's filled with laughs and a few life lessons.

I dedicate this book to my parents, Christine Simpson and Richard Simpson, and my kids, Cole and Savannah. I also dedicate this book to all of my training partners and professors. I mention many of them in this book, but there are so many more. Specifically, I would like to thank professors Wellington "Megaton" Dias, Luciana "Luka" Dias, Matthias "Mateo" Meister, Eddie "Doc" Lirette, Marco Macera and Micah Lopez. These mentors and friends are the black belts who have allowed me to grace their gyms. Finally, I dedicate this book to my editor and longtime friend, Lisa Cerasoli, who's inspired me to write through her own works and kept me on point.

Special thanks to…

Rick Brady and his company
UMICHIONE for their contribution in
making this book possible.

UMCH**ONE**
J I U   J I T S U

Foreword

Matthias Meister
Jiu-jitsu Black Belt NOLA BJJ

DRIVEN BY PERSONAL PROBLEMS AND A CHANCE ENCOUNTER WITH A Dravidian challenge, Michael Simpson was losing faith in the youthful belief of God-given physical power to reach super human-like abilities in extraordinary situations—like in a bar fight, a chance encounter with some hells angels, muggers, bank robbers, molesters, a grocery store line jumper. Not until he meets the trained skills of his seventeen-year-old cousin does Mike realize how off-whack that belief system was-and that there may be more to him than what nature or God given to him. In his case, he was an out-of-shape office tool, a designation that many men in their mid-thirties identify with and have accepted as fact or fate.

When Michael Simpson walked in to my Brazilian jiu-jitsu studio in New Orleans back in 2009, jiu-jitsu had already morphed him into a different person. He had reached the very respectable rank of purple belt. The purple belt is an important mark in jiu-jitsu because it is only obtainable through hard work, blood, sweat and usually tears. Simply put, it is proof you have achieved formidable skill at this game.

In Brazilian jiu-jitsu, unlike some other martial arts, superficial skills are not gained from slicing the air with a whoosh or breaking boards with hands and feet. Proficiency is only achieved by grappling with fully resistant partners. Since it takes years to program the brain to memorize body movements, fighting combinations, and even set ups, this craft can only be mastered by investing hundreds, or even thousands of hours. Training for ten years before you reach black belt level is not uncommon for a jitsuka.

Walking into a new Brazilian jiu-jitsu gym wearing a belt like Mike's means usually one thing; you will have to prove you're worthy of it the first time you spar. Mike showed up with his purple belt and a certain swagger that comes with achieving that stage, and passed this friendly challenge with ease.

In no time, Mike became more than a well-respected student and purple belt at NOLA BJJ; he became a part of the school and a very close friend of mine. Recently he surprised me with the fact that he was writing this book about his journey into jiu-jitsu. I was extreme-ly flattered when he asked if I'd write the foreword, but also slightly intimidated. But Mike is such an enlightened and interesting charac-ter; I discovered that this was a piece of cake. He's an open book who's full of fantastic foibles. And his ability to take it all in stride has endeared him to me—well, that and the satisfaction I've acquired from watching him grow as a human and a grappler.

This is the true story of a man in turmoil who finds his Zen through the sport of Brazilian jiu-jitsu. This is a common experience for those who study the art seriously—they find their Zen. They just don't "talk" about it much, and even fewer write about it. But trust me when I say that the knack Mike has for telling us his story, and taking us through his roller coaster ride of a personal journey, could not be more original. I think it's too cool that he's decided to unleash all of his angels and demons all over these pages.

I know Mike will reach the coveted and awe-inspiring goal of black belt. He may not do it before this book is published, but that's just another reason that I love the guy; he's finally figured out that it's all about the journey. It's not the destination. After a while it's about doing the work, every day, every month, every year, for life. The color of the belt doesn't really matter after all. The color of a bruise matters; watching that bruise heal matters. And then going back on the mat to do it all over again, well, that matters most of all.

Prologue

With my heart pounding and my mind racing, I stand on the edge of the mats poised to enter this arena of combat. The thing that got me here, the reason exactly, has slipped my mind by now. Other men and women around us are engaged in this game of human chess, busy disposing of their opponents via chokes, arm bars and leg locks or purely because of superior stamina. A gesture from the ref towards me and my opponent signals "the moment of truth." As soon as my foot steps on the mat, all my surroundings start to blur. As I enter a conscious state of trance, my only reality becomes the man across the mat from me. I look at him but don't see him; all I see is the outline of a stranger that has come here to meet me in battle. I see a silhouette that plans to twist my arms, choke me or pin me into a state of submission before I do the same to him. I have no emotions about him as an individual, no anger, no fear, no compassion—I am here to measure my skills in the art of hand-to-hand combat against his. Another gesture and a short command from the man presiding over our encounter encourages us to engage. Our ten-mile stares are now accompanied by circular pacing in an ape-like manner as we look for the opportunity to dominate. Upon first contact, all the jerking, pulling, pushing and twisting brings us crashing down on the mats in a mass of entangled arms and legs. And within seconds it becomes a systematic and highly skilled quest of obtaining inches. We try to gain inches on one another, so we may achieve the upper hand in this game of human chess that we call Brazilian Jiu-jitsu.

My mind passes in and out of semi-consciousness in regard to my surroundings. I see the audience and hear them, but they are just a backdrop. I see my nemesis, the referee, the score cards, the coaches, I see myself but it's all in the semi-consciousness of my mind, which is racing a hundred miles an hour while trying to exploit his mistakes before I make my own. I see ten moves that I need to accomplish to dominate, while I have to be aware of twenty other techniques that he can throw at me. Time creeps by. But Time, and Place and all of the people cheering and watching anxiously—and even the ref—are not part of our reality anymore. Our world has morphed into a surreal, singular game of winning and losing. It's become a primal quest of superiority of one man over another for reasons that I cannot remember at this moment. The endless seconds drag begrudgingly into minutes and pass us by in a measure of time that's only ever been acknowledged internally by us grapplers. The rest of the world can know nothing of this kind of time.

And then it opens up, the opportunity, the chance to expose my opponent's momentary lack of concentration, his failure to foresee my next move, his mistake. I expose it and "kill" him quickly.

And as suddenly as it had all begun, it is over.

The world around me bursts open in HD! Euphoria almost overcomes complete exhaustion as I get up, and with a hand out-stretched toward the man I just dominated, I help him to his feet. We smile at each other and suddenly I see a person in front of me, a brother of sorts, somebody I share a passion with, a passion for a sport that at-a-glance may seem primitive and even brutal. But upon examination, this sport opens doors, both inwardly and to the world around, like nothing I have ever experienced before. This state of mind, this persona that jiu-jitsu creates for me and for thousands of other practitioners is warrior-like: strong, wise, aware. This sport does not let the emotions of an event dictate a reaction to it. But instead the knowledge acquired through years of jiu-jitsu practice is used to predict the next move with cunning efficiency, simply to, at the end of it all, show nothing less than compassion and sympathy for my foe.

In these brief moments of sparring, I find something inside of me possessing superiority, not over man, but over mind and matter, over my own mind and physical body. That is the reason I am here challenging myself, that is what I am seeking to gain: dominance over my own manly limitations, so that I may grow above myself in the face of a challenge. And whether the outcome is winning or losing, maybe it'll lead me to the warrior within.

—MATTHIAS MEISTER

Chapter 1

Jiu-jitsu is like being a Jedi knight.
The knowledge is with you all the time—
you dream it when you sleep, you can see it walking,
it surrounds you. You go out alone but you are not alone
because you have jiu-jitsu.
—Olavo Abreu

A Fighter's Heart:
One Man's Journey through the World of Fighting
By Sam Sheridan

Batman

ON AN EARLY THURSDAY MORNING ON MARCH 21, 2002, EMPLOYEES OF Rental Services in Phoenix, Arizona arrived at work to discover that someone had stolen their thirteen ton dump truck by driving it through the chain-link fence surrounding the property. They reported it. Within a matter of minutes, police spotted the dump truck driving west, quite erratically, down Interstate 10. And so they began their forty-five minute pursuit.

At the wheel was ex-con Kenneth Ray Thomas.[1]

Several local television stations began live broadcasts of the dramatic chase. The ex-con eventually lost control and swerved at a police cruiser, causing the dump truck to overcorrect, resulting in a minor accident. This was enough to cause the police to back off of the chase and pursue the felon from a distance.

Doug Click, president and owner of Arizona High Lift, watched the scene unfold on TV before leaving for work. Within moments of clicking off his television, getting into his car and proceeding in the direction of the office, Click approached the intersection of Bethany Home Road and Central Avenue, just as he did every day. But today, his mundane trip to work was interrupted by the stolen dump truck heading north—which was in the process of running the red light. A westbound car—not realizing the truck had plans of running the light—ended up hitting its midsection. The rear wheels of the thirteen ton stolen truck drove over the car's hood like it was a prop at a monster truck rally. This interaction caused the dump truck to careen into the intersection signal pole. The dump truck's momentum coupled with the awkward collisions carried it another 150 feet and twisted it onto its side before it came to a metal-grinding halt in the middle of the arterial roadway.[2]

Based on the wreckage, Click thought that the thief surely must be dead, but instead, Kenneth Ray Thomas sprang through the broken windshield of the dump truck in full sprint like he hadn't obtained a scratch. Concerned that Thomas would highjack another car or enter one of the nearby residences, Click grabbed the baseball bat—that just so happened to be riding shotgun—and set off in pursuit of this criminal.

According to Click and media accounts, Thomas attacked Click with a pair of bolt cutters and Click struck back with the bat. "He was high as a kite. So, I cornered him, I pushed him so hard against the gate that it broke the latch (it was a pedestrian gate into a neighbor's yard). I hit him across the face with the bat. I grabbed him and hit him four of five times in the back of the head with the bat, and by that time, the cops had come up. I kneed him a couple times in the thigh, and he was screaming he was going to kill me. I was just laughing at him." [3]

The police took Kenneth Ray Thomas into custody. He was ultimately charged with a seventeen-year sentence. There were priors.[4] Meanwhile, Doug Click ended up being interviewed by *The Today Show* and other media due to his un-officiated involvement.

During one of his flurry of interviews, he earned the nickname, Batman.[5] It came out that Click was a Brazilian jiu-jitsu practitioner and had done some cage fighting.[6]

This drama occurred about a mile away from my home. Like Doug Click, I watched it unfold live on the morning news. And like the public at large, I stayed glued to my TV set until the chase resulted in a successful criminal capture. But I was in wonderment of this random man who took on a deranged criminal. The question had begun to plague me: what made "Batman" tick? Unbeknownst to me at the time, our daughters shared the same classroom. But it wouldn't be until several years later that our paths would finally cross.

Chapter 2

"I'm tough, Creasy," Pita demanded.
"No such thing as tough. There's trained and then there's untrained.
Now, which are you?" Creasy responded plainly.
—"Man on Fire"

Not Trained

In 2002, like Pita, I thought I was tough. But I wasn't tough. I was not trained. This lack of training caused me to question my own manhood, which led me to act with an unnerving and awkward sense of bravado at times. Yeah, I was a real stud. But I'm pretty sure I was the only person who was buying into even a fraction of the bullshit that I was peddling. Still, my amplified ego, however inauthentic, was the only tool that I possessed to mask my fear. And watching Doug Click kick that criminal's ass on live TV only reminded me that I was a puny, unprepared, fat ass yuppie. And that deep down I knew I would not have done what he had done. Why? As I watched the breaking news story I couldn't help but be reminded of an incident that had happened a few years back which solidified my theory, the theory that I was unprepared-not trained.

I was hanging out in downtown Tempe with my girlfriend one

Friday night when suddenly this dude did an Olympic medal worthy dash right in front of me. Within seconds, cops flew by, too. The thing is, I saw them all coming out of the corner of my eye. I could have stopped the criminal. A simple trip would have flattened the guy. When I say simple, I mean all I had to do was take my size twelve foot—and with little to no physical effort on my part—hook his ankle and the perp would have gone down in a heap. I am being about as sincere as you'll ever hear me be right now. But I didn't swing my leg into his path. I stood there stifled by the action. My brain didn't catch up with the action in time. I was alone with my thoughts and my fears. And my bravado didn't do shit; it was suddenly nowhere to be found. Imagine that? My lack of effort that night is something I will never forget and always regret.

Two years later in the spring of 2004, I promised my seventeen year-old cousin, Garrett, that I'd take him and his two buddies to Rocky Point, Mexico for spring break. Rocky Point was only a four hour drive from Phoenix. It was a no-brainer that I be the one to take them on that trip. It required no part of my brain to get them there, and I'm here to testify that I used very little of that same brain throughout the course of the vacation, or that entire period of my life. I was thirty-six, separated, and headed down that slippery slope to divorce without a crash helmet, a seat belt or even a goddamned manual. Shit, the anger would hit and there'd be nowhere to hide. I'd go to the gym, then leave angry. Then I'd hide out at the bars, but stay angry. Ultimately, I'd pass out in a fetal position somewhere, anywhere in my apartment—unconsciousness was a temporary relief—but then I'd wake up angry or sad or both. My apartment? Even thinking about that phrase, "my apartment," made me fucking angry. I hadn't had an "apartment" since college. I was well into an early mid-life crisis. Yes, those exist. I was overweight (fine, fucking fat), on a private whirl-wind tour of "Crazyland,*" depressed, irrational, lacking self-esteem (see: "fucking fat" above) and I was on my way to Rocky Point, Mexico with three teenagers. In summation, I was not an ideal chaperone for these boys.

*Crazyland is a place where anyone going through a divorce must pass. There are no exceptions. If you are getting divorced, your passport will get stamped in Crazyland, it is the law. You cannot reroute your trip to avoid this stop no matter how sane you attempt to be. My advice: get in and get the fuck out. The longer you stay, the less chance you have of ever leaving.

Evidence that you might be residing in Crazyland may include, but is not limited to:
- Over indulgence in alcohol and/or drugs.
- Over indulgence in sex. Men could have accidental encounters with fat chicks while wearing skinny jeans. Middle-aged women could suddenly have their ass crack peeking out from between the waist of a pair of low-rise jeans and their muffin top.
- Tattoos suddenly appear out of nowhere.
- Jumping out of, or off of, any fast moving object indicates that you're in Crazyland. And…
- Traveling to Mexico for Spring Break in your thirties— which is where we are in this story—is a red flag that

you're there. You might even be the honorary mayor at that point.

On our second night, I took them to Manny's Beach Bar.

They were not the only high school students at the bar that night. Other deranged chaperones/parents had brought their own children to the bar as well, mainly and more specifically, they had brought their teenage girls. The place was crawling with young girls. In the center ring of Manny's Beach Bar/Dante's Inferno, were high school kids trying real hard to look like college students. On the outer ring of Manny's Beach Inferno were the parents/chaperones pretending not to be affiliated with their high school kids, but keeping a close eye on them, nonetheless. My teenage boys, who earlier that evening graduated from Santa Ynez High School and were studying pre-med at UC Santa Barbara, had set their sights on three girls who were together, too (we guys like to keep it simple). But, Mom, was c-blocking that situation. So, they did what any teenage boys would do: they asked me to go hit on Mom, so that they could make contact. I looked over at her. The first thing I noticed was the ass crack, and then my eyes glided upward and settled on the tramp stamp. Ah, a fellow Crazyland tourist. This was going to be an easy kill. I went to work.

While I was busy martyr-doming myself, one of my boys got pretty drunk, strayed from the group plan and started picking up on a thirty-something biker chick named Red. Her name is of no importance; just that it was a fitting name and she looked the part. Red was at Manny's with four American Gangster types who did not appreciate the balls, ingenuity and efforts my personal teenager must have possessed to even think he could pull off a stunt like that. Words started to fly fast. Now, I am a pretty big guy, as I mentioned earlier, not huge, just tall, 6'3" and thick/fat. Usually my size is enough to deter an actual fight. However, there were four of them and there was just me and my three teenage boys (one of whom was stumbling drunk). Garrett and his sober buddy stood by my side while I yelled and chided one of the bikers. Despite what I wrote earlier, I wasn't exactly scared at that specific moment. This was probably because I was there as the "adult;" I knew it was up to me to take the brunt of this situation. And, this sort of thing happened in Rocky Point a lot. So, I interjected myself with relative ease into the disharmony happening at Manny's. I had been in fights before, even beaten up in Mexico, and I had survived that. This seemed to be another typical Rocky Point story that I could add to my heavy collection of them.

But at the peak of the argument—just before it elevated from silly to outrageously silly—I took a beat and glanced over at my two sober, seventeen-year-olds. They were standing tall and quiet and seemed to be consumed by a silent confidence. That threw me. I thought for sure they'd be shitting their pants. Huh? Then I noticed that the bikers were noticing them, too. It wasn't but a minute after that the two bouncers stepped in and encouraged all parties involved to move on. We all complied willingly. The bikers really surprised me with that. But, of course, while I had only a quick chance to glance back at Garrett and his buddy during this close encounter, it occurred to me that they were staring at them the whole time. Three months later I learned why my boys were consumed with silent confidence; they were trained.

# Chapter 3

"Jiu-jitsu, first lesson's free."
—Unknown

No Such Thing as Free

On July 4, 2004, I was with Garrett and my Uncle John at his ranch in Santa Ynez, California. I was done with my MBA and much closer to finalizing my divorce, which was my one-way ticket back out of Crazyland, or so I thought. In actuality, my soon to be ex-wife had gone to Mexico with new friends—friends I didn't know. This was no girl's trip. The thought of this drove me nuts and made me miserable. I felt sick and lost. I had used the excuse of the holiday to retreat to my Uncle's ranch; this favorite uncle from my youth. I was so sad and he would talk to me and didn't mind that divorce was the only conversation I had in me. Everyone would go to bed and he and I would sit by the large stone fireplace in his living room sipping on Jack Daniels and I would unload everything. He would listen and tell me where the separation was going but at the same time give me hope. He would simultaneously help me try to get Sarah (the ex) back and prepare me to be single. He knew I would be single but helped me chase this ghost anyway. He allowed me the folly without judgment.

The entire time on the ranch was not depressing divorce conversations. I had my two kids, Cole, who was three, and, Savannah, eight, there with me. We ate like kings, with Central Coast tri-tip steaks, sodas and beer; and activities including swimming, shooting and horseback riding. In the middle of all of this bi-polar roller coaster of emotional peaks and troughs, on one enjoyable afternoon, Garrett asked me to roll.

To "roll" is a jiu-jitsu term practitioners use for wrestling, with the bonus feature of submissions (chokes and locks) replacing pins. No punching is allowed. Once caught in a submission, the victim can make it stop by "tapping out," either verbally or by simply tapping on the opponent's body or the ground, or by yelling "Tap!" while tapping the opponent. In my case, I cried, "Uncle." Memories of my childhood rushed in—memories of my big brother torturing me—and "Uncle" naturally came to mind. Fortunately, it was effective.

Being fresh out of my MBA, I did a quick SWOT (*Strengths, Weaknesses, Opportunities and Threats*) analysis on Garrett's request to roll. This is what I surmised:

Strengths:

• Size: Looking at my cousin, I felt pretty confident. He was seventeen and close to seventy pounds lighter than me.

• I never competitively wrestled, but in addition to my big brother "practicing" on me for sport, he regularly solicited his buddies to do so as well. This was non-stop. I knew I could defend myself.

• Conditioning: I ran a couple miles every morning. I thought that meant I was in shape. (This should be going under weaknesses.)

Weaknesses:

• I had watched the first Ultimate Fighting Championships, and had seen the sorcery of Royce Gracie*. Therefore, I wasn't totally sure I could foil Garrett's attempts for submissions.

Opportunities:

• I had taken two years of jujitsu (jujitsu is different than jiu-jitsu) in college. It was a combination of judo, aikido and karate. It did not include grappling. The aikido portion did give me a few wrist and arm locks and the judo gave me some throws.

Threats:

• Garrett and my Uncle John's faces were branded with similar knowing smirks after I agreed to roll. There was that. And, as the poker saying goes, "If you walk into a room and can't tell who the sucker is, it's you."

The fight began. Within seconds my limited judo experience was nullified as Garrett pulled me into his guard. This move is where the jiu-jitsu practitioner pulls his opponent on top of him and to the ground.

---

*Royce Gracie was the UFC Champion in the first UFC. His family is credited with taking Japanese Jiu-jitsu and creating the form known as Brazilian Jiu-jitsu, which is also now commonly known as Gracie Jiu-jitsu.

Being on the bottom in jiu-jitsu is not considered a disadvantage. So we're on the ground and I'm on top of Garrett, which seemed like an "okay" position to me, but before I could think about my next move, Garrett's legs were wrapped around my head and neck. I was in a triangle choke. I tapped. He released the hold. We reset. The whole event lasted less than thirty seconds. If this had been a fight to the death, that would've been my last thirty seconds on earth.

Like the vast majority of people this happens to, I believed it was a fluke. Garrett got lucky. So, we restarted and I went at him like a bear fighting for a salmon. It played out exactly like the first time. He went for the technique known as an arm bar. An arm bar is a technique used to attack an opponent's elbow by locking his arm in place, usually between the legs, and pulling the joint backwards. In less than a minute, I tapped. He had theoretically broken my arm and killed me. I still didn't believe. I wanted another rematch but I couldn't breathe; I was gassed. Garrett kneeled in front of me. He didn't even look winded. It looked like he had just dashed up one flight of stairs. Maybe. Meanwhile, I looked like I had just completed several iterations of Hell Week training and didn't survive it. He allowed me to regain my breath. Thankfully, it only took three more "killings" in front of my kids before I became a believer. I left the barbecue with the lesson firmly planted in my mind. Thirteen years of school, a degree in civil engineering, an MBA and the greatest lesson I had ever received was from a seventeen-year-old kid who wasn't trying to teach me anything at all. He was just doing what he had been taught to do.

This repetitive public display of affliction solidified further the notion that I was trapped in "Crazyland." I knew I wasn't the only person to ever go through a divorce, but this kind of lonely—mixed with disproportionate amounts of fear and bravado—was making me come off like a jackass on a pretty regular basis. And I was never the jackass in my former married life, or in my former single life before that. I was the guy everybody liked and turned to for advice. You could talk to me and trust me. I told good stories and people naturally looked up to me. If memory serves, I think that was called "having your shit together." Yeah, that was me. This guy now? The one who just had his ass handed to him over and over again in front of his children? This guy sucked. He lost his family, and his dignity wasn't trailing far behind. And for the first time ever, I felt like a quiet, cowardly spectator lurking in the shadows, witnessing my own demise and doing nothing to stop it. I wasn't "aware" of these new surroundings. That was one problem. I wasn't capable of handling the jackass brewing inside of me—that was another. And I wasn't worthy of being anybody's hero. I was nobody. And now my kids knew it, too. And that was the biggest problem of all.

Live with that, Jackass. The words kept reverberating in my head. *Live with that, Jackass. Your kids know you're a loser. They just witnessed it.*

But I couldn't live with that. Unfortunately, this event made me realize I wasn't on the mend, but rather white-knuckling my way right into the heart of "Crazyland." The crash landing was in clear sight, but digging my way out of the inevitable wreckage didn't seem to be an option yet.

Chapter 4

"For the choke, there are no tough guys;
with an arm lock he can be tough and resist the pain;
with the choke he just passes out, goes to sleep."
—Helio Gracie

Some Party

ON MARCH 22, 2012, IN GRAND RAPIDS, MICHIGAN, BRANDON Slanger—a schizophrenic recently released from jail—walked into Mike & Spike's Party Store and attempted to rob it by stating that he had a gun in his pocket. Just about the time Slanger was making his demand, college student, Iraq veteran and mixed martial artist, Zack Thome, unwittingly got in line to purchase his usual handful of miscellaneous groceries. The man in line behind Slanger turned to Zack and urged, "Go ahead."

Zack still didn't quite get it.[7] The man, who was now standing more safely behind Zack whispered, "I don't know, I think he's got a gun."

Zack, being a regular, knew the cashier. In Zack's words he later reported, "I look at the cashier, I kind of know him, I come there every day. I whispered to him, I mouthed to him, 'Are you getting robbed right now?' he said, 'Yeah,' like really scared."[8]

In a flash, Zack attacked the criminal with a rear naked choke, pulling Slanger backwards and to the ground. Zack set the choke in tight. Within seconds, Slanger was unconscious.[9]

The point of a proper rear naked choke it to do exactly what Zack accomplished—cut off blood supply to the brain and cause immediate unconsciousness. Anyone who has trained long enough has been "choked out," and knows this. For those who don't, being choked out happens as follows:

1) You struggle as your vision narrows.
2) Everything goes black.
3) When the blood does return to your brain, you awake as if from a nap, except generally more confused.

This hold, more commonly referred to as "the sleeper hold," has received a bad rap over the years as it has been used by the untrained and resulted in death. In actuality, in practiced hands, it is an effective way to subdue an aggressor without bashing them bloody and stupid. To make my point, every year there are at least 100 Brazilian Jiu-jitsu tournaments around the country, each having between 100 and 3,000 competitors. At each of these tournaments, one to three people get choked out because they don't tap. And not one death or injury has ever resulted to date. The trained practitioner knows it only takes seconds and you must release the hold quickly to restore blood to the brain.

Zack was trained. His mixed martial arts taught him how to grapple and set a rear naked choke. His military training taught him to isolate the threat. In this case, the threat was the potential of a gun in Slanger's pocket. In another interview after the incident Zack said, "The actual tactic of the choke was what I learned from Grand Rapids Mixed Martial Arts. I want to stress that the Grand Rapids Mixed Martial Arts is probably the reason why I had the confidence to do something, for sure. As far as protocol for isolating a person of interest and making sure there's no threat that was from the military. So as soon as I had him on the ground, it was like snap, snap, snap from what I learned in the military for apprehending a suspect." [9]

What the person who doesn't train in jiu-jitsu or mixed martial arts often fails to understand is that when you train a lot, you can see a person's energy. You know their size and can "feel them" prior to engaging. You can even predict their reactions to your actions. Through training with different sparing partners, some larger, some smaller, all shapes and sizes, you build a mental menu of body types. Without thought, a jiu-jitsu practitioner or mixed martial artist will notice subtleties like ears; cauliflower or pristine? Other appearances like facial hair and tattoos mean virtually nothing when it comes to engaging in a fight. Of course, long hair or a big beard might be an extra handle, and a martial arts tattoo might mean you have your hands full. However, typically, these are masks for fear, insecurity and uncertainty.

In another interview with *Fox News*, Zack stated, "I can't just let this whole thing happen. If he got away with the whole thing I would feel guilty, like I could have done something, but I didn't. So I really only had one option."

In watching the video, Zack was an articulate college student and regular looking guy. You wouldn't have looked at him and thought "fighter," except that his left ear had a simple "tell," because it was mildly cauliflowered.[10]

Chapter 5

"These bruises make for better conversation."
— "Bruises" by Train

Bruises

I HAD JUST RETURNED FROM MY FOURTH OF JULY TRIP WITH THE KIDS TO Santa Ynez, or as I remember it, my first jiu-jitsu lesson at the hands of my seventeen-year-old cousin, Garrett. I shot through my front door, tossed the keys, walked straight to the fridge and grabbed the Phoenix *phone book* off the top of it. Yes, in 2004 people still used that thing called a phone book. I rummaged through it and found Megaton Brazilian Jiu-jitsu. That was that. I memorized the number, literally, and picked up the phone. A lady with a very thick Brazilian accent answered. My first experience with Brazilian culture was beginning. Brazilians speak Portuguese, but when they speak English it sounds like they're yelling at you. So, this Brazilian lady is yelling the class schedule at me and sounds extra pissed off when she adds, "Jiu-jitsu: First lesson is free!"

I arrived to class on a Saturday. The class was being run by a black belt named Mike. He was nice and lent me a gi. In layman's terms that's a karate outfit. The classes began with a thirty minute warm up, followed by something called sweep-pass-the-guard, then a thirty minute lesson and then it concluded with forty-five minutes to an hour of rolling.

My first day was a blur. I was physically cashed in by the end of the warm up. Sweep-pass-the-guard is like rolling, but there are no submissions. The goal is essentially to grapple for top control. It's a little more detailed than that description, but you get the gist. I had already wrestled for half an hour after the warm up and by the time the lesson had begun, I was mentally broken. I couldn't tell you what I was supposed to have learned, just that I was grateful for the rest period they gave us, and I was dreading the shit out of the final hour. During that last hour of rolling, I picked up right where I had left off with Garrett, except that my partners didn't seem to like me. I fought with every ounce of my soul, which added up to three minutes of soul. After that, I spent fifty-seven minutes getting willingly throttled.

My mistake was that I didn't tap fast enough. My ego wouldn't let me admit defeat. I rolled that first day with white belts, and because I was initially thinking that they couldn't have known much more about the sport than I did, I tried too hard and didn't tap soon enough.

The belt order from beginner to expert in adult jiu-jitsu is white, blue, purple, brown, black and finally red. (Memorize this list, it will come up repeatedly.) Red belts are rare. It's like receiving a Lifetime Achievement Award (and I think you must have the last name Gracie).

Because I did not tap fast enough, my elbows became badly inflamed. When class ended, I literally staggered to my car to drive home. Two blocks from class, "home" was no longer an option. The pain in my arms and elbows was too great to steer the wheel. My ex-wife's house was close and pain killers were on the top of my list of immediate needs.

I plowed in uninvited and made a bee-line for the couch. I landed on it as if I had just taken my last step and, coincidentally, the couch was right there to cushion the fall. The next natural position my body took without permission was the fetal position. I began shouting orders at my ex, calling out for the strongest pills she had, and ice, lots of bagged ice, or frozen anything.

After Multiple ass kickings on the mat, and now public humiliation (it doesn't get more "public" than your ex seeing you like this), you'd think a smart person would have cut his losses. I mentioned that I was an engineer with an MBA earlier, right? Yeah, I figured I did, jackass that I am.

Two days later, I returned to find that Megaton, the operator of the jiu-jitsu gym, had made his way back from Brazil. The warm up was simple, just some sit ups and pushups. That was a relief until the purple belt who was leading the warm up declared, "Circle up! Six-minute abs!"

Minute one was a standard crunch, my abs were holding on, no problem. When minute two rolled around we flutter-kicked with heels six inches off the ground.

"HEADS OFF THE MAT!" Megaton's Brazilian accent boomed across the small gym.

You're fine. You are fine. I kept telling myself. But as my abs started to fail, the phrase changed to, *Fuck six-minute abs.* You really are a pussy! And it didn't revert back to you're fine. This inner monologue just kept getting nastier and nastier. About four minutes in, my neck decided to replace my abs as "wimpiest part of my body." The pain was unbearable. How the fuck has it been holding up my inflated head all these years? It was an honest question. Meanwhile, Megaton had picked up a pointer stick and was walking on top of our bellies, hopping from person to person and whacking us every now and again. I looked to my left, then my right. He was way across the room on top of another sucker. *Jesus, I'm going to pay for this shit.* I knew that much. But I took my chances, stopped crunching and let my head hit the mat.

"SEEMPSON! DON'T YOU WANT THEE SEEX-PACK ABS FOR YOUR GIRLFRIEND?!" His thick accent echoed across the gym. I jumped back into crunching. After two more minutes of sheer agony, the class proceeded as usual…with me getting my ass kicked.

In order to explain the next hideous experience in my small, small world, I must briefly explain the jiu-jitsu move known as the "guard" or "Gracie guard." If you're in someone's guard, he is on his back and you're inside his legs. (To further visualize this move think of the traditional missionary position with the person in the guard being the guy and the person pulling guard being the chick.) So, I was in someone's guard, and as they went for a move, their legs squeezed very tightly around my floating rib, causing it to separate from the its buddies. It was excruciatingly painful, with the added bonus of lingering long after class ended. When I, for example; coughed, sneezed, laughed, breathed, farted, wiped my ass, or tried to reach my alarm clock, I was in excruciating pain. The alarm clock was the most fun. I literally had to roll over in the opposite direction (away from the clock), then onto all fours and crawl back toward the clock. Think about how annoying the average alarm clock is anyway. Now imagine it's this unreachable entity. Or, imagine that just as it goes off, a fist magically shoots down through your bedroom ceiling and punches you hard in that floating rib. I officially owned the meanest alarm clock ever. Those were my mornings for a month.

On August 21, 2004 I took my staff on an office trip to Las Vegas to see UFC 49. The headliner was Randy Couture versus Vitor Belfort, and the undercard included Chuck Liddell. At the time, these guys ruled the underground world of Mixed Martial Arts. Chuck is a Santa Barbara native who fights out of my hometown of San Luis Obispo, California. I had been a moderate fan of the UFC since the late '90s, but now that I was two months into my own practice, I was fascinated by the sport.

We stayed at The Stratosphere. The group was a mix of the staff at my engineering firm and their significant others. We left work early Friday afternoon for the five hour trek to Vegas. Saturday, just before noon, we met out at the pool for a friendly match of Ping Pong and some drinks. It was Vegas, baby. It was also getting hot, so I took off my shirt to jump in the pool, and that's when everyone burst, simultaneously, into a very specific kind of laughter. It was that gut-holding, knee-slapping, finger-pointing laughter. And it was directed right at me. I had completely forgotten that my torso and upper arms were covered in quarter-sized bruises of every color of the rainbow but with a heavy emphasis on indigo and green. I looked like a severely battered child…at least, that's what I was hoping. I mean, I'd hate for my buddies to think some chick had done this to me. And, I was way too bruised to pull off the "we were just getting kinky" argument.

Almost instantly after the laughter had faded into an echo and traveled up into the sunny Vegas skies, my employees gained an immediate and clear understanding of what this trip meant, and the moment turned briefly solemn. Yeah, it was brief, we were still in Vegas, but it was indeed solemn.

But for me something lingered. For the first time the word "reborn" no longer sounded stupid, or like it was reserved for religious fanatics. It crept into my consciousness and latched right on. My body was shedding its skin. The old me would soon be a thing of the past. Both my mind and body were morphing slowly and painfully (so painfully) into someone new. Was it someone who might be able to handle hardship, change, divorce, finger-pointing and a real fight better than that guy I used to be? Hopefully. Was I ready to say good bye to everything I knew? To the guy who'd been comfortably inhabiting my body for the last thirty-seven years? Fuck, I didn't know. But looking down at the splay of bruises decorating my body as if Jackson Pollock went apeshit with scads of paint and a dozen brushes made me aware of one, simple fact: I could never quit or stop practicing jiu-jitsu.

I couldn't go through this twice.

Chapter 6

"Warriors are not the ones who always win,
But the ones who always fight."
—Wellington "Megaton" Dias

Why is he "Megaton?"

WELLINGTON DIAS IS A BRAZILIAN WHO IS IN HIS FORTIES AND HAS BEEN competing in jiu-jitsu and judo since he was four years old. He's famous, well-liked and most importantly, respected in jiu-jitsu circles. Wellington earned the nickname "Megaton"— which by definition is a unit of power chiefly used for nuclear weapons equal to one million tons of TNT—because of his judo training and propensity to launch his competitors high into the air like the blast of a nuclear bomb. While he may have received his nickname from when he was younger, and from tossing competitors around, he has recently added durability to his reputation. Jiu-jitsu World Champion, Roger Gracie, once wrote an opinion piece on the best jiu-jitsu competitor in the world. In it he stated, *"If it had to be one person, you have to look at Wellington "Megaton" Dias as he has been going for such a long time, way before I got my black belt. He doesn't always get gold, but he is still there fighting, often in the adult division, showing what he is all about.*

This guy is a better competitor than me.[11]

One night I went to train and there were two new guys, Russian brothers. They were big, ripped and fairly cocky. We went through our warm up and into sweep-pass-the-guard. I was quick to notice that they had more than beginner skills. When it was time to roll, Megaton took up a position on the wall with a timer and watched over us. As we entered into the second roll, one of the Russians challenged Megaton.

"Why do you only watch?" he demanded, "Why do you not roll with your students?"

Megaton casually told him that he will roll with them on two conditions:

1) They both have to roll with him for ten minutes each. And...
2) The mouthy Russian brother must go second.

And so the games began. Even though I had only been around a short while, I had never seen Megaton go at someone like he went at these two guys. Within the first minute of the ten minute roll, Megaton had submitted the first brother at least four times. During minute two, Megaton didn't exactly submit the Russian; he put him in horrible claustrophobia inducing positions and sadistically held him there instead. Before the third minute rolled around, the brother was tapping like crazy and wanted to quit.

Megaton held steady and barked, "No! You owe me eight more minutes!" and proceeded to dismantle this guy while his mouthy brother looked on in horror. Then the brother took his ten minutes of hell as promised. Except this time it looked so much worse. Apparently the more taciturn of the two Russian brothers was just the opening-act. Having rolled with Megaton several times, I had been stuck under Megaton before and held in those positions and it sucked and I was a respectful student. Nobody ever saw the Russian brothers again.

On another occasion years later, I was leaving the noon class when Megaton asked me to join the evening class. He said the school had received a disrespectful call from a guy who called himself "The Silver Kid," and he wanted a good turnout when this guy arrived. Apparently, The Silver Kid had made big claims about his athleticism, stating he could do a thousand pushups without stopping. He also said a broken finger was all that had kept him from Olympic wrestling. Then he questioned how a guy as small as Megaton could offer him much of a challenge at all. Megaton walks around at roughly one hundred fifty pounds. This was a show I did not want to miss. I went home and discovered that on IMDb The Silver Kid had quite the extensive list of feats.[12]

I arrived late. The warm up was in full swing. As I dressed out, I glanced around and did not see The Silver Kid.

Megaton was working out the squad pretty hard when he spotted me. "SEEMPSON! Did we sleep together last night?!"

I stammered, "Wha...ah, No?!"

Megaton shot back, "Then, why you don't say, 'hello?'"

Just then, a guy in a red gi came running out of the back, joined the group and saved me from further berating. It was the Silver Kid.

We finished the warm up and went into sweep-pass. I couldn't tell what was going on with The Silver Kid, but by the time we finished, he had vanished again.

Megaton belted out, "Ah, Seelver Keed! Where are you?! You are going to mees the lesson!"

The Silver Kid was in the bathroom throwing up.

"You aren't tired, are you?! You can do a thousand pushups!" Those two sentences danced off Megaton's lips and echoed throughout the dojo.

The Silver Kid returned and the lesson proceeded.

Luka, Megaton's wife, rolled with the Silver Kid. We all watched as he got submitted over and over by Luka. She's a world class black belt, but given The Silver Kid's ego, a woman kicking his ass seemed to be emasculating. Then, during the second roll, The Silver Kid left again due to fatigue this time. Megaton called him back out to roll with a small purple belt named Dave. Dave destroyed him. Let me make this point: neither Dave nor Luka were disrespectful; they just applied relentless technique, which drove home the point that The Silver Kid's arrogance was disrespectful.

He was angry and frustrated and told Dave that the gi was stopping him from performing as well as he might. So much for the point-making; Dave agreed to shed the gi. The two began to roll no gi.* Dave again submitted The Silver Kid. They restarted. Dave dropped a triangle choke. The Silver Kid punched him. Dave responded by holding the choke just a little longer after The Silver Kid tapped. This led to a

---

*No gi is done with shorts and usually a rash guard (which is like a tight T-shirt).

loud argument. Since The Silver Kid wanted to punch, Dave offered to put MMA gloves on (or not) and have a real fight.

The kid declined.

The night finished with the school lined up according to rank, which is a rarity. Megaton made some announcements regarding classes and then stated plainly, "You should all remember if you are going to talk the talk you better be able to walk the walk."

The Silver Kid came back one more time…and then never again. Funny, his experience at Megaton's never made it onto his IMDb page.[12]

Chapter 7

"The painful warrior famoused for fight,
After a thousand victories, once foiled,
Is from the books of honor razed quite,
And all the rest forgot for which he toiled."
—Shakespeare

Know Your ABCs?

ON AUGUST 15, 2012 AT THE ABC STORE ON FREEMONT STREET IN OLD Town, Las Vegas, two men began arguing at the entrance. They appeared drunk as their arguing intensified to swearing and shouting. Tourists were milling about at the souvenir shop. The lady at the counter approached the two and asked them to leave. She noticed one had taken a drink from the cooler without paying and she confronted him about that, too.

That same evening James McSweeney, a transplant from England, had taken visiting family and friends to experience Freemont Street. If you've never been, Freemont Street is a tourist destination and contains the Golden Nugget Casino as well as Binion's. The entire street is enclosed and covered in a myriad of lights which put on a continuous show. There's also a zip-line that spans the length of the place which people pay to ride every minute on the minute. It's quite the spectacle.

McSweeney's sister and niece had entered the ABC Store to look for some souvenirs. He opted to wait out front. After a moment, he couldn't help but notice the two men as he stood idle.

McSweeney later described the scene in a radio interview stating, "Two guys had kind of started to argue. And they're arguing kind of really aggressively, they're swearing, and the place is packed full of people and kids. The lady came out from behind the register and tried to grab the drink off of the guy and said he'd stolen the drink from the shop. And as soon as she grabbed it, the other guy ran around to the back of the register, opened it and got the money. As she went over to jump on him, the guy went in and he pulled a knife out."

With his family trapped inside the store with a knife-wielding criminal, McSweeney did not hesitate. He followed the criminal, grabbing the knife and sweeping the assailant face-first onto the ground. Using the knife he'd just snagged off of that guy, he held the second guy at bay while holding the first guy on the ground.

McSweeney is an MMA fighter. He fought in the UFC and was on the UFC reality show "The Ultimate Fighter."[13]

"I didn't even think about it to be honest. It's just a crazy thing that happened in town. I didn't even think it was that big of a deal. But if it shows that MMA guys out there, that we're trained professionals, we can do what we can do. We can handle situations and help. It's better to paint us in this kind of light, than in a negative light where they see that we're bad people, or we're aggressive, cause the real people know we're not."

The second assailant ultimately fled. And when security arrived they were not too happy about the condition of the first man on the ground...until they saw the knife.

Chapter 8

"Life is trouble.
Only death is not.
To be alive is to undo your belt and look for trouble."
—Nikos Kazantzakis, Zorba the Greek

Batman Returns

AFTER GOING TO A UFC EVENT WITH ME, MY FRIEND AARON (THE OUT-of-high-school wrestler at my job) joined Megaton's class. Due to his extensive high school wrestling career, grappling came naturally to him. He did not like the gi, however, because the gi slows down the wrestler. Aaron preferred to train on no-gi nights. I began to do the same, too, as it was harder for people to kick my ass once I shed the gi. Don't get me wrong I was still getting crushed it just took a little longer before I tapped. I also switched up nights because, well, I was plain curious to see Aaron grapple.

One night a guy approached me to roll. He was shorter, but thicker and likely weighed more. Because we were training no-gi, that also meant there was no belt for me to see his rank. The guy dismantled me in seconds. I threw everything I had at him—which was some muscle I had acquired by doing pushups at the end of my runs to impress my "chick of the month"—but he was stronger and more skilled. And despite the strength differential, he was using technique to dominate me. I rolled some more, because I'm no quitter and a glutton for punishment, but eventually I tired and moved to the wall for a break. Immediately preceding my series of foibles on the mat, the same guy asked Aaron to roll. Apparently he didn't require a break against the wall to catch his breath and stabilize his shaky frame. What a dick.

Aaron took the guy's back pretty easily. I was thoroughly impressed until I saw Aaron tapping. What the hell happened?

I leaned over toward the guy next to me, "How did he just tap Aaron?"

My fellow wall-holder-upper told me that Aaron had taken his back, but crossed his legs, which led to an easy submission. Then he adds that the guy is Doug Click, like he was someone I should know.

It felt familiar, hearing his name, but I couldn't figure out why. "Who's Doug Click?"

"Remember that guy who chased the guy who stole the dump truck? He's that guy."

Shit. I definitely knew Doug Click. He was, after all, one of the reasons I was here.

Later that week when I was talking with Sarah, my ex-wife, I told her that the guy who chased down the dump truck thief was in my jiu-jitsu class.

"You mean Doug Click?" She uttered, just like the guy from class, like I should know him. "Yeah, his daughter goes to school with Savannah. They're in the same class. His wife is super nice." Then she casually adds, "He's very tough, Mike, be careful."

It seemed like Sarah had taken some kind of secret pleasure in knowing that Doug Click had kicked my ass, was kicking my ass and would continue to kick my ass at various times in the future. It turns out that "Batman" was a purple belt under Megaton.

At the next class, I formally introduced myself and mentioned that our daughters went to school together. We talked for awhile, like dads do, about our kids and what not.

Like his wife, it turned out that he was super nice, too…except when he was rolling.

Chapter 9

"Sometimes it hurts to win,
And sometimes it feels good to lose.
And the prettiest color that I've ever seen,
Was found in a bruise."
—"Big Tension" by Blaine Long

Black Eyes

In early December of 2004, Megaton Academy had its annual Christmas & belt promotion party. This was my first experience at a Brazilian steak house. The two greatest exports of the Brazilians: jiu-jitsu and Brazilian steak houses. Clearly Brazil is a man-dominated place consumed almost entirely by fighting and red meat. If you've never been to a Brazilian steak house, they're all pretty much the same. They're your standard dimly lit steak house with a salad bar hidden somewhere in the back of the joint for good measure (at least that's what they had told me). But, at Brazilian steak houses, each table has a cylinder that is half green and half red. If green is showing, they bring meat, all types and cuts of meat: steaks, chicken, chicken hearts, sausage, lamb, pork and the list goes on (but, trust me, you don't want to hear it all). And, if the cylinder is red, they stop bringing out meat and return with a defibrillator. No shit.

Both my kids, Savannah and Cole had begun doing jiu-jitsu as well, so I decided to bring them to dinner. Sarah wanted to go, too. It was sort of an awards ceremony and she wanted to be there in case the kids received something. I picked everybody up. Immediately Sarah looked at my eye and smirked. (Yeah, it was swollen and bruised purple and black.)

"Jiu-jitsu?" she said, pointing at it as if she might poke it.

I responded with a nod. She retracted her arm, thankfully. I wasn't in the mood to start off the night with a jab. Fortunately, my eye looked painful enough to satisfy her.

It was my first black eye in years. I wasn't sure how or when it had happened, but after five months of training, I had quit trying to figure out how the bruising occurred.

We walked into the restaurant and straight to Megaton's table where I introduced my family. When Megaton looked up and smiled we all noticed that he, too, had a black eye—that somehow made the nagging pain in my eye subside. I guess that's the definition of male bonding or some crap.

We grabbed some seats at a nearby table with my new buddy from the dojo, Jeff. He was a purple belt who had taken mercy on me. By that I mean he had begun to actually teach me technique, rather than continuing to just kick my ass. I liked Jeff. I noticed he, too, had a black eye. And suddenly I felt very cool, like I was part of a club, like a Fight Club. Although, my physique was still in closer sync with that of say, Meatloaf's, than it was with Pitt's or Norton's, it seemed this eye of mine somehow made me an honorary member of this secret and prestigious guy club, at the very least. This, whatever this was, was more than male bonding. Our "Fight Club" went beyond that, it was extreme. I never thought of jiu-jitsu as something that would reshape anything more than my body, but it did.

I joined because stress had started chomping at me pretty regularly. It was thinking of taking a permanent bite right out of my ego, I could feel it. I felt puny, weakened by life. I was out of shape, lethargic and negative. I joined so that I could be like the Doug Clicks of the world. Batman had its perks. Batman made the news. Batman was a stud. But it never occurred to me that Batman could be a member of "Fight Club" until now. Being an individual is all everybody preaches about these days: be yourself. But tonight I didn't feel like myself, not my old self anyway. There's something bigger going on in the world of jiu-jitsu, and it has nothing to do with self. My black eye just might be the official "invite" I had been waiting for.

At the time, my big project at work was the Phoenix Light Rail system. My firm had a portion known as Line Section 3. We were doing traffic related design and the maintenance of traffic plans during construction. Every two weeks we had a meeting with our section lead along with the lead design firm and local government planners and officials. The project was just finishing when I had begun jiu-jitsu, so they had really only known the pre-jiu-jitsu married Mike. This new Mike was a little disturbing for them, I could sense it. For starters, "this new guy" was in the middle of a divorce. And now this soon-to-be-divorced Mike was coming into meetings with black eyes and various other marks and scratches on his face, arms, hands. This guy was sore and bruised. He was also more relaxed in general (see sore), but he had a big edge now. Married Mike was edge-less. Married Mike was soft and smiley. It would have been one thing to be going through the divorce, or just taking up jiu-jitsu, but it was the definite combo that brought on such a severe reaction to my new persona. I wanted to assure them that I was evolving into an improved version of me. However, seeing as how my Visa just kept getting extended in Crazyland, it was hard to pull that off completely. You see, I silently dug the quiet attention. Once I realized what was going on, I almost craved it, thanks to Crazyland. Walking into a meeting with a black eye and watching people muffle their reaction gave me pleasure. Observing my coworkers wanting to speak up, but afraid to ask any questions was sort of thrilling. With the exception of a few cocky dudes who'd make some sly remark insinuating my wife was responsible for my new look, everyone attempted to be more discreet. And that was a laugh and a half, accusing my wife of beating me up. (If you had ever met her, you'd know that.)

My response to the banter was simple and to the point. "I took up Brazilian jiu-jitsu."

To which they would always then ask, "Is that like cage fighting?"

"Yeah, something like that."

I kept it concise and let their minds fill in the blanks, knowing that whatever they were imagining was way worse than what I was actually doing. Either way, though, they weren't even close to getting their minds around this evolution I was going through. How could they? I wasn't even there yet. Evolving on the outside came fast, or faster. It's the rest of the work, the work I didn't even know about that was going to come slow into my consciousness. If that wasn't the case, the jack ass in me would have vanished by now. But there he was, keeping his answers short and vague and allowing the curious apprehension of my coworkers to linger inside the walls of my work place. But something else was beginning to brew that would eventually change all that.

I was calmer, and not just because I was whipped from a class the night before and slept hard despite the frozen veggies piled on top of my beaten body. I used to walk into meetings with a chip on my shoulder, ready to argue and fight, like I had something to prove. Now, I was humbled. I knew I was not tough, that there were so many people out there who could kick my ass, and some of them even did, regularly. My eyes had been opened up to something special, something every man ought to know about. But at the same time, I was still glad they didn't; I quietly held onto this secret, like I was the only one with key to the universe. *Jackass.* Whatever.

In a meeting, voices would rise like they always did, like two dogs barking across a fence…but I was no longer one of the rabid dogs. I saw the barking for what it was: insecurity. And I had nothing to be insecure about because these dogs had no bite. Now the fence that I had jumped to get into jiu-jitsu, those dogs bit. They bit until they drew blood. They ripped the flesh right off, sometimes to the bone, at least that's what it felt like.

I was feeling this metamorphosis more and more everyday and this new quiet confidence needed to be tested, but not by the office dwellers. Megaton was always pressing us to enter tournaments.

Initially, the concept just seemed completely silly, a grappling tourna-ment. That's for high school and college kids, not yuppies. And yet, I could feel the draw, the pull into this unknown place.

Chapter 10

"The art of living is more like wrestling than dancing."
—Marcus Aurelius
Roman Emperor and Philosopher

The Million Dollar Man

I~t was the July 7, 2012 issue of~ *The New York Post* ~that had an~ article entitled "British Jiu-jitsu Expert Grabs Central Park 'Purse Snatcher' Before New Yorkers Could Lay a Hand on Him." Part of the article read as follows:

> *This guy ought to register his hands as lethal weapons. A tough-as-nails jiu-jitsu expert made such quick work of a purse snatcher in Central Park Thursday, a group of other would-be crime-stoppers could only stand by and watch his martial artistry.*

The word *tough* in this headline made me grin; it's like the word *free*. These words have ceased to exist for me. Nothing is free, someone always pays for it. Even the free hot dog at the car dealership makes it into the price of the car. Or, a free week of jiu-jitsu—that came with a world of pain. For some it came with a lifetime membership into that world, and you pay your dues till death, that's the plan I was on. And there is no such thing as tough. There's trained and then there's untrained. And everyone, even the trained, can be broken. In the case of the Central Park purse snatcher, the hero, Gaston Cavalleri was trained. He blogged about the incident:

> *Please consider I heard two girls screaming, and one started to cry, while screaming "HELP!" I wasn't going to l e t that go down in front of my face and walk away from it.*[14]

According to the newspaper article, which came complete with a photo, a sixteen-year-old kid ran off with a middle-aged woman's bag containing her cell phone, credit cards, money, keys, you know—her life. It was grabbed while she and her friend were lounging on a grassy area around 8:30 in the evening. Gaston was nearby and took off in immediate pursuit, along with several other good Samaritans. But Gaston caught up with the crook first and brought him to the ground. Using Brazilian jiu-jitsu, he detained the thief and held him, single-handedly, until police arrived. From the photo, it looked like he had used a variation of a rear naked choke. His legs were wrapped around the thief while one arm coiled around his neck. According to the article, the purse snatcher complained about not being able to breathe, and that's when Gaston "politely" adjusted the hold.

The assailant was not beaten up. Jiu-jitsu allowed him to detain the suspect, not pulverize him. Gaston had told authorities that he didn't want to hurt him. He wanted to secure him, so that he wouldn't run away.

In the end, the victims were happy getting their belongings back, and the sixteen-year-old was charged with grand larceny and possession of stolen property. And, he was not beaten bloody by an angry mob of good Samaritans, but merely detained.

Gaston Cavalleri has an interesting back-story in that he grew up poor in England…and then his family won the lottery. He's been traveling and writing ever since, and took up jiu-jitsu while living in South America.[15]

Chapter 11

"If we can breathe we can fight.
And we can breathe so we can fight!"
—*Pat Tillman Story* by Riche Wolfe

Getting Better

ON APRIL 22, 2004, PAT TILLMAN WAS KILLED. BEING AN ARIZONA STATE graduate, I was a huge fan of Pat's. When Pat Tillman and Jake Plummer were both picked up by the Cardinals, for the first time— and the last time ever for any sport—I bought season tickets. His death depressed me, which felt silly because I had never met Pat Tillman, not once. Later that year, I bought the book authored by Rich Wolfe about Tillman's life. It was a collection of stories told by those who knew him. The "quote" is from one of those stories. It's what Pat screamed at his teammates after losing to Jacksonville. My mind latched onto it, and the phrase sticks with me when I train.

When you're untrained in a fight you will use your muscle to the point of exhaustion. Ever run a mile in six minutes? Ever run a six-minute mile while breathing through a straw? Right. *Who would do that?* Well, when you're gassed and a full grown man is putting his knee deep into your belly, that's what it feels like. A person will tap just to take a full breath of air. You're drowning, panic hits, the mind searches, all the toughness you thought you had bleeds out and you tap, or you die. So, it's the simple things that help you survive at first. Sometimes something as simple as a quote reminding you that you can breathe, and therefore you can fight is all it takes. And in order to continue to fight you must conserve your energy, so that you can continue to breathe and thus continue to fight.

My first real feeling of victory came one evening while training no-gi. A new guy came to practice. He was big, probably 230 pounds and he looked to be about thirty years old. When the buzzer went off, I immediately pulled guard. He went up into a stance that I had only experienced with wrestlers. His hips were high in the air and his legs were wide apart. He moved a lot; he was quick. He made short work of my guard and passed into side control. For the first time in jiu-jitsu, I recognized a pattern and a sequence. He was a wrestler with no jiu-jitsu experience, which meant that I could regain my guard just by doing a simple hip escape. I noticed that when he had passed my guard, he left his arm and head in between my legs for a moment. My mind told me that he was ripe for a triangle choke. So I did just that: I hip-escaped, recovered guard and anticipated his next move. Then he did exactly what I had modeled in my head. He passed identical to the first time. I dropped the triangle choke on him. He tapped.

We rolled a few more minutes until the round was over. Then I sat next to Megaton against the wall to rest and recover. "That guy was a hand full; definitely a wrestler."

The guy resting on the other side of Megaton chimed in. "You could say that. He used to wrestle for Michigan State."

And then Megaton smiled and said, "Yeah, but you triangled him, Simpson, you triangled him." With his thick Brazilian accent that sentence sounded more like, *Yah, but you tree-angled heem, Seempson, you tree-angled heem.*

The moment felt so good. I sat there and quietly relished in it. I'd been training my brain to pay no heed to the victories, or stew over the defeats. That wasn't what jiu-jitsu was about. That wasn't why I was there. But, I don't know…this felt better than good. Sensing the connection between mind and body, predetermining another person's next best move, that was all new to me. It was a breakthrough and a monumental moment. Looking back, I'm glad I did; because by the next round, this other new guy kicked the living crap out of me.

Another victory early in my training—before tournaments came into play—was during an afternoon session. Lunchtime classes were easier to attend because I was so busy with my kids in the evenings. Megaton showed up with three beefed-up, long-haired, tattoo-covered bikers who marched in wearing Hells Angels' jackets. *Why would Hells Angels train jiu-jitsu?* That was my first thought. Megaton answered that question before it left my brain—because he's Megaton and probably a fucking mind reader to boot. Anyway, the story as I understood it was that an Arizona Boxing Commissioner had had ties to the Hells Angels. The commission was interested in seeing if jiu-jitsu tournaments should be sanctioned boxing commission events. (This story is consistent with recommendations made in a 2000 Arizona Office of the Auditor General report [report 00-018] which recommended that the legislature and commission consider regulation of nontraditional contests and amateur contests.)

So, three Hells Angels shed their jackets and each put on a gi. I was a bit stunned. One was a really small guy, quite muscular, but small. I took no particular pride in kicking his ass, but the other two were regular sized dudes. I choked and tapped all three in no time. No such thing as tough, just trained and untrained. *Remember?* The small guy took to the sport and came back to train pretty consistently. Shit, for all I know, he still trains. The other two never came back. I sucked at jiu-jitsu. I mean I sucked badly, and I tapped out three Hells Angels…in a row. I tapped out society's tough guys.

The Hells Angels at Megaton's school did not come without controversy. Megaton asked me what I thought of them training at the school. Apparently, a police officer who trained there gave him the "them or me" ultimatum. He refused to train with convicts. But there was no denying it for me; I really enjoyed taking it to them. And I could have enjoyed that every week. So I didn't care where they trained. Plus, if they weren't with Megaton, they could easily have found another place. And Megaton teaches honor and respect, as well.

After the class, I immediately called my ex, who was waiting in an airport security line. I knew she was headed out of town, but I was so pumped I had to tell the one person who would at least pretend to care.

She picked up.

I blurted, "I just choked out three Hells Angels at Megaton's. I mean I kicked their asses! Don't get me wrong, they didn't have knives or guns, so take it for what it's worth. But I kicked their fucking asses!"

It was one, big, long sentence. There was no "Hello, how you doing, honey (or ex-honey)?" anywhere to be found inside all my fast-paced enthusiasm. I felt like a kid.

"Holy crap!" Her tone started strong. She sounded engaged and excited for me, too. I think she even giggled. "Well, yeah, it probably would have been different if they'd had a knife or a gun."

Suddenly I heard a TSA announcement blare into the phone like it was meant just for me. "Ma'am, you can't say 'gun' in a security line!"

"I gotta go!"

…And she was gone.

When I first showed up at Megaton's, the goal was to never get my assed kicked again, or so I thought that was the goal. Then one day it occurred to me that jiu-jitsu was so much more than that. I was dealing with divorce. I was living in Crazyland. I was out of control. Sometimes the emotion of the divorce would hit me so hard it felt like a choke hold that wouldn't let up no matter how many times I tapped. And then came anger. It became a close friend of mine; we were attached at the hip before jiu-jitsu. I didn't want that "thing" as my friend or in my life, it didn't even suit me, but I couldn't shake it, or dodge it and I didn't seem to have the ability to compartmentalize it. The only time I felt free of it was when sadness took over, lucky fucking me. My family, as I had defined it, was a thing of the past. My kids? I always missed them, even when I was with them. I would be with them and actually feel the pain that I knew I would experience in the near future, once I walked out the door. That pain would show up pretty regularly before I was even gone.

And my wife, I missed her, too. My mind vacillated between missing and resenting my one, true love. Basically it was all overwhelming. Every damned thing in my life was extremely overwhelming. And I didn't talk about it much. I mostly made a series of poor decisions—before jiu-jitsu that is—because I'm a dude.

Before jiu-jitsu, I would go out and run and run and run, sometimes until I puked. The psychology of the running made me feel like I was running away from the problem. But when I ran, I was still thinking about my problems. There was no escape from my own mind, and when I returned from the run the anger and sadness were still with me. Apparently I was being chased by those fuckers. Other times, I retreated to a bar for the escape. That never worked, in case anyone's wondering.

As soon as I found jiu-jitsu, I had found a place that was not a bar. And it wasn't a long run till I puked. This small room with a padded floor and padded walls had become many things to me: my church, my therapist, my gym. When I rolled there was no time to think about problems. When a man is trying to choke you, there is no time for running through all of the bullshit of the day. There is only one task at hand, kill or be killed. The insanity and the desperation of the six-minute round quieted my mind. I was too tired to be angry or sad, and the endorphin buzz created after rolling, whether I was killed or not, left me feeling elated. So, after two hours of mind-quieting six-minute intervals, my mind was reset like a computer that was rebooted. I would leave the gym and all of my problems and emotions seemed to stay there, like the sweat that was left on the mat and in my gi.

Chapter 12

"Do or do not, there is no try!"
—Master Yoda

Hairdresser on Fire

BACK IN 2002, I HAD RETURNED TO COLLEGE FOR MY MBA. IT WAS AN executive program at Arizona State and required a number of formal business events. My wardrobe was lacking, so I went out and bought better business attire. I'm a hands on engineer—which has always resulted in me getting dirty—therefore I was never much for suits. As a matter of fact, I spent the first two years out of college working on a drill rig. Back then, I thought it made me tough. It didn't. It just made me dirty.

A couple of years later, I obtained that MBA. Shortly thereafter, my divorce became final. Somewhere between those two life-altering events, I had started jiu-jitsu. I still didn't know shit about the art, it hadn't seeped into my bones yet the way a bitter cold wind does when I start on an early morning run. It didn't feel natural, like breathing. I was still weak and clumsy and cerebral. Mostly, it hadn't occurred to me that jiu-jitsu was doing anything for me, other than turning me into a mass of aches, pains and bruises. Basically, it was serving as a constant reminder of my status as a pussy cat in a world consumed by lions. And this was tough, but I had yet to find a permanent escape route out of Crazyland and jiu-jitsu was my break from it. Yet, all that aside, I had somehow managed to nab myself a hot girlfriend, who was also nice enough. And so a cruise seemed like the perfect way to celebrate this colliding of several non-related events; the divorce, my MBA degree, nabbing a hot girlfriend, etc. Okay, see that? That's Crazyland talking right there. We'd only been dating a few months, me and my new hot girlfriend who was "nice enough," why would I think a cruise would be the way to go?

She was a hairdresser, so naturally we hit it off from the onset. (No, we did not.) The only cruise I had ever been on was for my honeymoon which had been over a decade earlier, so this was going to be weird. And I'm here to tell you, my hand to God (or jiu-jitsu), that engineers probably shouldn't date hairdressers as a general rule. Or, at the very least, they shouldn't hit the open seas together for a week. The following conversation will explain my thinking on this. We were sitting on the upper aft deck bar. I was deep in thought and she was talking about something—the latest pop star or hair products, or who the hell knows....

"You aren't paying attention to me. What are you thinking about?"

"You really don't want to know."

Smiling excitedly, she squealed, "Sex?!"

"No, not sex," I smirked and reiterated, "and you don't want to know."

With a big toothy grin, she responded, "I do, I really do!"

"Fine. You see the canopy above us? Well, each corner is being held by twenty-two, one-inch diameter bolts. You see them? And the ship is traveling at twelve knots. But in a storm, like a hurricane, you could have 100 mph winds, plus the wind generated by the twelve knot speed of the ship. So some engineer calculated that it would take twenty-two bolts to resist this incredible force. But, what I am wondering is, how strong is the canopy fabric? Because I bet that shit would tear before—"

"You're a fucking nerd! Seriously, shut up and try looking at my tits!"

My hand to God (or jiu-jitsu), that's what she said.

Anyway, we left the upper aft deck to dress for dinner. I had not worn the clothes I put on since graduation. Two years of the executive MBA program meant a regularly catered classroom, which meant my pants were a bit snug the last time I had worn them. Now, nine months of jiu-jitsu made my pants not only fit again, but they were loose. Nice. The problem, however, was with the button-down. My double chin was in full retreat, that much I had noticed, but my neck had apparently "adjusted" to the six-minute abs. My neck was really fucking muscular. I could not get even close to buttoning the top button. I had to go to the ship's gift shops and purchase a new shirt.

My body's gradual morphing was becoming increasingly more evident.

I found a shirt that fit and we had a nice dinner, I guess. But the rest of the cruise felt pretty much like that first conversation. Basically,

all of the conversations that ensued that week were a general reenact-
ment of that first conversation about hair products, the speed of the
ship, rock stars, ship revenue at sea versus revenue in port, her tits,
water displacement versus weight of the ship, her tits. We subjected
ourselves to same circular conversations for a week straight while
afloat in a boat.

It was tantalizing. (No, it was not.)

I returned from "my adventure at sea" to find a message from Garrett
awaiting me. He was coming to Phoenix for The Arizona Brazilian Jiu-
jitsu State Championships. He wanted me to sign up to fight. Four
months earlier, I had lost my one and only match in a tournament. I
feared having a career all the way to black belt without any wins.
Despite that, I signed up anyway. Thanks to the cruise, my weight class
was Super Super Heavy. (They should just call it The Fat Ass Division,
I really don't know why they don't.) This weight class was for 221
pounds and up. I was 240 pounds at the time. I was a fat ass.

My first match was uneventful, other than alleviating the concern
of living the rest of my jiu-jitsu life without a victory. My 260 pound
opponent shot a takedown; I stuffed it and worked my way to a
mount. Given that he was 260 pounds, the word shot is probably an
overstatement. The match ended with me mounted on top of him,
which gave me a four-to-zero win.

My next match was a 250 pounder with tattoos all over his shiny,
bald head. As we waited in the bull pen, I made a Seinfeldian crack
about something random. He grunted and glared. No sense of humor
there. On the mat, he, too, shot for a single leg takedown. Again, I

stuffed it, but my knee inadvertently smashed him in the nose, which seemed to be even less amusing than my joke. *That's fucking karma, buddy. You should have just laughed at my joke.* The match was halted so that the cut could be bandaged, but it was deep and wouldn't stop bleeding. The referee declared me the winner. I won by default. But the match had lasted four minutes before it was called, so I was tired. The tournament organizers gave me fifteen minutes to rest before the final match. My daughter and son were sitting next to me while Garrett was helping me stretch my grips. A lot of the time when you fight in the gi, your grips (the muscles in your forearms) become extremely fatigued because you're always grabbing and holding your opponent.

My nine-year-old daughter was so excited from the back-to-back wins, she was downright giddy. "No matter what Dad, you're going to get a silver medal!" She squealed while dancing in place.

Looking down at the pool of sweat that had rolled off of my head and gathered at my feet, I responded, "Yeah, fuck that, I think I'll go ahead and win the gold. I may never be here again." Then I patted her on the head and walked onto the mat.

I did not look at my opponent. *If I can breathe I can fight. If I can breathe I can fight.* The ref signaled for the match to begin; we gave each other a quick high five and began. My opponent immediately opened up his gi. To this day, I still don't know why. *Maybe to show me his six pack?* Then he grabbed me and pulled guard. In the world's most boring match, the rest of the time was spent with him keeping me in guard as I attempted to pass. While this was going on, I heard Megaton's wife, Luka, along with his daughter and several of my teammates yelling and cheering. People were actually cheering for this thirty-seven-year-old chubby yuppie. Holy shit. And then I saw my son and daughter sitting Indian style on the edge of the mat. They were screaming like crazy, too. Seeing those two little kids cheering for me was worth every ass-kicking I had ever received…and the thousands more to come. That moment had brought me straight out of the "match trance" that had always occurred, but I refocused with an even greater awareness of what had to be done to win that fight. I passed into my opponent's half guard, which was enough to get me a win. The gold medal became mine that day. I left the tournament with three wins in all. Now that could get me through the rest of my life. It doesn't matter if I ever win another jiu-jitsu match.

For the first moment in a long time, I didn't feel like a loser. I finally felt something new—despite all of my imperfections and all of my flaws, I felt perfect in the moment.

Later that week I went over to my girlfriend's apartment. I showed her the video of my tournament and I brought my medal, too.

She was antsy while we watched. I couldn't tell if she didn't like the fighting, or didn't get it, or didn't care. When it was done, she said, "I have a video, too!" and put in some porn without making a single comment about my matches.

I was disappointed and torn. I mean, as a man who's been working to improve and getting his ass kicked quite regularly as proof, I wanted at least a pat on the back for my accomplishments. But as a dude, I was under obligation to the unwritten, unspoken understood number one rule of porn: if it's on, you have to watch it.

When we finished screwing, she went to the bathroom to pee, so I switched out the porn for my fight. It was a harmless move, or so I thought until she came dodging out. She took one, long, angry look at the TV and went up in flames. "What the fuck is wrong with you!? You would rather watch that instead of porn?! Instead of fucking me?!?!"

Maybe she thought I was some sort of narcissist, but that wasn't it. During the first viewing, I had noticed that I had missed several opportunities to pass my opponent's guard. As a matter of fact, this was exactly what I was pondering during the sex fest. And now the cat was out of the bag.

Needless to say, we called it quits. Six months later I still had jiu-jitsu, though. And not only did I have it, but "we" had decided to take our relationship to the next level. That Christmas I got my blue belt from Megaton.

White Belt Accomplishments:
   One and a half years of training ✓
   Ass kicked (again and again) ✓
   Humbled ✓
   Black eyes ✓ ✓ ✓ ✓ ✓
   Bruised and battered ✓
   3 Tournaments ✓ ✓ ✓
   5 Wins ✓ ✓ ✓ ✓
   2 Losses 👎 👎
   1 Gold medal ✓
   1 Bronze medal ✓

Self-esteem on the slow but steady incline ✓

Nearly 1,000 hours of jiu-jitsu logged ✓

Six pack abs for my girlfriend ✑

Girlfriend ✑

240 pounds and holding... ✑

One-way ticket out of Crazyland ✑

Chapter 13

*"The key to immortality is first living
a life worth remembering."*
—Bruce Lee

Bones

ON MARCH 16, 2011, A CAR PULLED UP TO THE INTERSECTION OF MAPLE and Walnut in Patterson, New Jersey, just adjacent to the Great Falls of the Passaic River. The tiny national park nestled in heart of Patterson was created in 2009 because of its historical significance due to the waterfall's industrial use in early America. The same falls were featured in an episode of the Sopranos where a drug dealer is thrown over the pedestrian bridge. I thought that was a fun fact. The faulted basaltic rock provides a seventy-seven foot drop for the majestic waterfall, which was the purpose and destination of the visitors.

UFC heavy weight Jon Jones and his two coaches, Greg Jackson and Mike Winklejohn were headed to the park for pre-fight meditation. Jon was the headliner for UFC 128 later that night. Part of Jon's pre-fight routine has always been to find a serene spot and meditate in order to associate with different levels of energy in nature. The hills, river and massive waterfall were a perfect location for this pre-fight routine.

As the coaches got out of the car, the driver warned them that the neighborhood was known for muggings. Jon sat there for a minute reassuring the driver that they were MMA guys and that they would be fine. Just then—as if to validate the driver's warning—an elderly Spanish couple came running up gasping for breath. The man darting away in the distance had just smashed through their car window and stolen their GPS system.[16]

Without thought, the two coaches took off after the thief at full speed. Jon, still buckled in his seat at the time of the story telling, got off to a late start. The perp headed up a hill on a residential street with closely spaced shotgun style houses. The coaches were gaining on this guy, but Jones had found his gazelle legs (or so he said), and breezed by.

"The next thing I know, I catch up to my coaches, and I am jogging and they're sprinting, and I am like 'so what are we going to do when we catch this guy?'"

Through gasps of air, Greg Jackson barks at Jon Jones to get back. Jon's got the fight to consider, but he ignores the demands of his coach and hits the jets.[17]

As Jon closed the gap to twenty yards, the shock of seeing Jones, maybe his speed, or maybe his size, caused the criminal to trip and fall to the ground. He tried to get back up but Jones flattened him out with a leg sweep. Greg Jackson pounced onto the scene promptly behind Jones. Jackson pushed Jones and yelled, "Get back! You have a fight tonight!" Then Jackson set an arm bar while Jones ignored his instructions and used a figure four technique he had learned in college in a criminal justice defensive tactics class.

A news clip showed the perp face down on the pavement with Greg Jackson mounted on his back and an arm held twisted behind him. Meanwhile, Jon Jones was holding the legs, one crossed over the top of the other. (Immobilizing the one leg keeps the other immobilized as well.)

Neighbors gathered around while Jones lectured the thief about stealing. Soon after, the police arrived and arrested him. One of the cops recognized Jones. If you're into the UFC, you're WAY into the UFC. The fans are fanatics. This cop was a fan. He turned to Jones astounded and uttered, "Don't you have a fight tonight?"

Chapter 14

"I fear not the man who has practiced
10,000 kicks once,
But I fear the man who has practiced
One kick 10,000 times."
—Bruce Lee

What's 10,000 Hours?

IN MALCOLM GLADWELL'S BOOK *OUTLIERS*, HE MAKES A POINT THAT TO BE an expert at anything it takes 10,000 hours of practice (the book is based on the original study by Anders Ericson). He used this theory to explain over-achievers such as the Canadian All-Star hockey players and Bill Gates. In short, excellence comes down to the time you put into the activity you're doing, or the 10,000 hour rule.[18]

Back in 1996, when I was twenty-eight years old and my marriage still felt like home to me—this was back when Crazyland seemed about as real as Oz—I had signed up for a jujitsu class at Arizona State University. *Jujitsu* is not to be confused with Brazilian *Jiu-jitsu*. (Look closely at the words.) Jujitsu, as taught at Arizona State University, was a compilation of judo, aikido and karate. Unlike Brazilian Jiu-jitsu, there was very little sparring. Beating up students is generally frowned upon by colleges.

So I was happily enrolled in jujitsu and talked about it occasionally at work with two new interns, Steve and Aaron, who came to us fresh out of the same high school. Well, we were chatting one day and Steve said he had just signed up for a submission grappling tournament. Both Steve and Aaron were former wrestlers in high school. Steve was state champ. But despite that, they wanted me to show them some submissions that I had been practicing in jujitsu. I think what we were all truly interested in knowing was if a wrestler could beat a person who studied martial arts, but Steve really wanted to have a leg up in the tournament, too. I think they both thought that wrestling prowess combined with some quick hands on training—practicing moves in the back laboratory area at work—would achieve that.

The tournament was being held at Phoenix Baptist Church on Central. Coincidentally, this was the exact location where Doug Click would later take down the dump truck thief (in 2002).

So they both knew I was learning jujitsu—Arizona State style—and wanted to know some submissions. I knew a couple. Reluctantly, I showed Steve a wrist lock and a Kimura arm lock. Years later, Brazilian Jiu-jitsu taught me more effective forms of both these moves.

I went with Aaron to support Steve. The tournament was organized in that there were rules, but it was early on in the modern version of the sport of submission grappling, so some entrants wore gis, some wore shorts and no shirt, some wore shorts and a T-shirt and others wore a wrestler's singlet. The coach from Phoenix College allowed his wrestlers to miss practice if they entered the tournament, so there were a bunch of guys in singlets waiting to grapple. Phoenix College is known as "FK" among college snobs. Wait for it… There it is… And laugh. (It's ok, the Phoenix College grads still don't get it, either.)

One guy showed up with a gi, though, a blue belt. The gi had a Brazilian Jiu-jitsu logo. This blue belt had a match before Steve's. He came out and submitted his opponent in seconds, then went to rest while waiting for his next match. Steve was up next. Naturally, he took a wrestler's stance inside his opponent's guard. The match went several minutes until the opponent reached up onto Steve's shoulders, grabbed his T-shirt and used it to choke him. Steve tapped and was done. The Brazilian Jiu-jitsu blue belt re-entered the mats and within seconds he tapped out an FK wrestler. In the final match, this blue belt met up with the guy Steve had lost to earlier that evening. He choked him until he was unconscious, winning his bracket. Then like a ghost, the blue belt was gone.

Watching the quick, clean successes of that Brazilian Jiu-jitsu blue belt throughout that evening made me realize how ineffective jujitsu (Arizona State style) really was. I went home and immediately quit the class.

When I read *Outliers* a decade later, in November of 2008, I was at the end of my blue belt career and it made me start thinking about how many hours I had put into Brazilian Jiu-jitsu. I estimated that I had approximately 1,000 hours of jiu-jitsu time in the year and a half between starting jiu-jitsu in mid 2004 and getting my blue belt at the

end of 2005. I logged 250 hours of mat time and 750 hours of thinking, studying and learning (videos and books).* Many jiu-jitsu practitioners admit to thinking about jiu-jitsu constantly. This concept pro-
liferates their Facebook posts, conversations, T-shirts and bumper
stickers: Eat, Sleep, Jiu-jitsu.

The Brazilian Jiu-jitsu blue belt who dominated the 1996 grappling tournament that Steve had entered into had likely had between
1,000 and 3,000 hours of experience. His limited jiu-jitsu experience
(limited according to Gladwell's theory) easily destroyed his lesser-
trained opponents, including the college wrestlers who had likely had
over 3,000 hours of wrestling experience. So, in bringing this concept
back to the news stories of MMA fighters, jiu-jitsu practitioners (and
Batman) bringing down the criminals among us, it began to seem not
so crazy after all.

*During the Cold War, the Soviets conducted a study using three groups of athletes:
one group did all physical practice, no visualization, the second group did three
quarters physical training and one quarter visualization and the third group did half
physical training and half visualization. These studies showed the best performance
in the third group.[19]

Chapter 15

"It's not wrong…you can use a hammer to chop down a tree,
But is it the right tool?"
—Megaton

Lunch Time Blues…and Belts

"Eet's not wrong. You can use a hammer to chop down a tree, but is eet the right tool?" Megaton said that to me one day while training, it was right after receiving my blue belt. He didn't like my technique choice.

I kept up with my lunchtime training sessions, not just because of all my kids' extra curricular activities, but also because it worked better with my new evening activity: chasing tail.

Just after receiving my blue belt, a core group of people began training with me at lunch, and I formed a bond with them that has lasted over the years. One guy was quite the character, his name was Mark Spray. Rarely did anyone at Megaton's Academy call him Mark or Spray, though. It was always Mark Spray. But his name was spoken like it was one word: Markspray. Megaton always hesitated as he said the name, so it always came out as "Oo-Ah-Markspray." For that matter, I was never Mike at the school; I was "Seempson." Markspray was in land development and real estate and he was very, very "Scottsdale."

Also around this time, I introduced a business client of mine to jiu-jitsu, his name was Eric Kaufman. As weird as this may sound, we called him Eric. One day at work, I picked up the phone to find Eric asking me about an old project. I hadn't talked with him in some time and in the process of catching up I told him about jiu-jitsu. He said he was a black belt in Taekwondo but wanted to try something new. A few weeks later, I walked into the dojo a little late for the noon class to find some dude running in a circle and grinning at me. It had been so long since I had seen Eric that I didn't recognize him. Plus he was in the wrong world, I knew him from my work world, it was all quite confusing. I remembered thinking, "Damn, that is a cocky new white belt all smiling at me and shit." A few weeks later we had a happy hour in Scottsdale with the team and I asked Eric if he liked jiu-jitsu.

He said, "Yeah, that shit will make a man out of you!"

The guy was hooked after one class. That must have been what the big smile was about.

Because Eric's name sounded like Aaron's name, Megaton was always shouting, "Mike's-friend-Eric!" every time he wanted Aaron's attention. He couldn't seem to get it right. Megaton had never once called me Mike, which made Aaron's nickname even more ironic. Aaron worked for me and so we would both cut out of work at lunch to train. It was nice to have a buddy, even though being a loner there for a while was fun, too. Eric, Aaron, Markspray and I were all similar in age and our professions were all related, so I think that commonality created easy friendships as well. I could trust these guys not to hurt me, for they, too, had to go to work after training. These guys became my new best friends. I had already had my college buddies, and now I had the guys I rolled with, these were my friends for life.

Now, even though I could trust this group, Jiu-jitsu did not come without injury and the spring of 2006 was loaded with them....

Megaton and Luka had started to prepare the team for the Pan American Championships. This is the third largest event in the sport. Markspray and Eric were both white belts at the time. I was a blue belt. The three of us decided to enter the tournament.

The week before the tournament, I was rolling with a guy we called CIA. I can't remember his actual name, but I just remember him coming into class and speaking Portuguese to Megaton and Luka, and then Spanish to some other people. When asked about his profession, it was a nondescript international business which required him to be gone now and then, thus "CIA." CIA had only one speed, which was kill (again, CIA). On this day, he did not disappoint, he was having trouble passing my guard and in one of his attempts he landed on my leg and it pulled my hamstring. I guess that's one way to pass. I was out for the 2006 Pan Americans.

While the hamstring was enough to keep me out of the Pan Americans in 2006, I had also begun to have knee troubles. I kept hearing a pop coming from my right knee. It didn't hurt, but others would hear it when we'd roll, too. A group of students from an affiliate school had come down from Oregon to train and get ready for the Pan Americans. While rolling with a guy Markspray had dubbed "The

Manhandler" my leg got hung up and my knee popped, but this time it was very painful. With Aaron's help, I made it home. It didn't hurt if the knee was completely bent, but it was impossible to straighten it out without feeling intense, excruciating pain. Three doctor visits and an MRI resulted in meniscus knee surgery that June. Recovery was short, but I could not stay away from the gym during that time. I would go sit and watch-just being at the gym made life right. Even if I couldn't get my training in (my therapy), the place had become my church and a place of camaraderie.

Chapter 16

"That which you manifest is before you."
— *The Art of Racing in the Rain*
By Garth Stein

Pan Americans 2007

TO TALK ABOUT THE 2007 PAN AMERICANS, I MUST START IN THE FALL OF 2006, at The American Nationals. My Uncle John—the same Uncle from the infamous Fourth of July barbecue that put me into this sport—had signed up for the tournament as well. Garrett had choked his own Dad out one too many times, and now Uncle John trained. Megaton was in the super fight and Markspray was competing, too. Even though there were only three in my division, I signed up for the 2006 American Nationals.

My Uncle brought his girlfriend. They were newly dating, she was about twenty years younger than him, and she was very pretty. As I warmed up in the bullpen, I watched my Uncle head out for his match. Uncle John was in his early sixties at the time; his opponent was slightly younger, mid-to-late fifties. However, his opponent was a lifelong grappler, a wrestling coach and the like. Well, that guy grabbed onto Uncle John, immediately put him on the ground and tore him apart.

Afterward my Uncle was embarrassed by his performance and said to me, "Never bring a girlfriend to a tournament. I was by the bathrooms kissing her when they called my name. I was soft when I got to the mat. Mentally, I was prepared for a hug, not a fight. And that guy grabbed me and threw me to the ground! There was no hugging. Never bring a chick to a match."

As funny as that was, he was right. How can a man be ready to engage in a combat sport when his mind is in a mushy state? After watching that spectacle, I vowed to never bring a girlfriend to a match.

For me the American National Tournament was a letdown as neither of my opponents who were scheduled to fight showed up. However, as I waited in the bullpen to see if there'd be a last minute addition, I watched in awe as this giant warmed up next to me. I studied him further until I was nauseous with clarity. *Holy Christ! What is that specimen?! He looks like he'd be in my age and weight bracket, I guess…but no, oh, no, tell me it ain't so?! Is that my opponent? How can I beat him?!*

The man was Jarrod Bunch, a former NFL running back for the Giants and the Raiders. Other notches in his Super Athlete Resume included playing football at Michigan, setting a world record in weight lifting at the age of sixteen and winning the 2002 NFL Tough Man contest. But he lost an MMA match to former NFL receiver Michael Westbrook via rear naked choke, which happened to be how he found this sport, too—by way of humiliation. Mr. Bunch is exactly one month younger than I am. That would be my age bracket. And he looked roughly twice my size, even though he weighed in at 265 pounds, which was my weight bracket. Shit. It's amazing what twenty extra pounds can look like when distributed like his was. Fuck. He was massive.[20]

In order to accurately compare our Super Athletic Resumes, it's important to highlight mine. Mine included senior year high school football on a one-and-nine team. I set a record that year for the most attempts at getting out of lifting weights.

While I was warming up in the bullpen, Markspray came up to me and asked if "Nine Toes" was my opponent. Jarrod Bunch used black electrical tape to adhere some of his toes together. This gave him the appearance of having nine toes and so that's what we called him. (Jarrod, if by chance you're reading this, Nine Toes was not a pejorative, just an observation, buddy.)

It turned out that I was not going to fight Nine Toes on that day at the American Nationals, he had signed up for a younger age bracket as it had more competitors. I still wonder if he had switched that up before or after he saw me? However, as intimidated as I was by his size and athleticism, part of me wanted the match. Anxiety twisted into disappointment inside my stomach. I wasn't an adrenaline junkie, I didn't even like heights. Yet, in spite of that, I learned to fly, even puked in a glider once. And I willingly threw myself off of—and out of—cranes, buildings and air planes. I had tried bungee jumping, sky diving, and cable dropping (700 foot drop off of the Sky Tower in Auckland). But this wasn't about adrenaline, it was about pushing myself out of my comfort zone to feel alive because the idea that death is in the hands of one piece of equipment failing is kind of thrilling. Okay, I might be a junkie. Well, for whatever reason, I wanted to test myself against Nine Toes. But that day at the American Nationals was not the day. I would have to wait.

This brings me to…

In March 2007, I was driving back to Phoenix from San Luis Obispo, California from a weeklong trip with my kids when I got a call from Markspray. Markspray had just signed up for The 2007 Pan Americans and wanted me to as well. The tournament entry window was closing at midnight. I had intended to sign up, but life had kept me busy. I'd forgotten. Excuses flew out of my mouth; I was out of shape, I hadn't trained in several weeks, etc. Markspray didn't accept any of them.

"Who cares? Listen, Simpson, we'll head out next week. I got a nice place rented on Hermosa Beach. We fight, we hang out on the beach, have some cocktails, meet some chicks."

In part, my excuses were true, but mostly, my fears and apprehensions about tournaments were dictating my hesitation. Plus, I had this eerie feeling that I'd be fighting Nine Toes, and I was not prepared for that. But who could argue with drinks, chicks and a beach?

The tournament was less than two weeks away, so there was no way to get in any hard training. I rolled relatively lightly and avoided CIA. I went to yoga to visualize victory. To beat a man like Nine Toes it was going to take Soviet-like techniques, minus the steroids. At the end of every yoga class the instructor wants you to meditate for a few minutes before you leave. I've always just finished my practice and left before the shavasana shenanigans began, but on this particular day I stayed to visualize how I might beat Nine Toes.

First visualization: We start, give each other a high five at center mat, he grabs and lifts me above his head and throws me, WWE style, into the bleachers. Okay….

Second visualization: Nine Toes jerks me around causing me to lose my footing, lands in side control, headlocks me into submission.

That was better, but not exactly what I was going for. Visualizations three-through-nine got progressively better until finally I visualized victory.

Tenth visualization: I stay on my feet for at least three minutes to fatigue his muscles, ultimately pull guard, faint with an arm bar submission and switch it to my bread & butter sweep-to-mount, which works and puts me up seven-to-zero…and time runs out.

I opened my eyes to find that this took so long that all the hippies had left class, and I was the last person in the room.

On my last training session before we left for The 2007 Pan Americans, Megaton watched on as Aaron and I rolled. Then he decided to keep score. Aaron went up on me by four points. Megaton shouted, "You need to do something, Seempson! You are losing! Thirty seconds!"

Aaron was in my guard, my eyes were closed, I had pressed the pace and could hear Aaron breathing hard, I moved my hips out, shoved his head and dropped in an arm bar, and he tapped. Even though I had not trained hard, I felt I had a real chance at the Pan Americans because my game felt good and I had gotten my mind right.

Markspray and I drove out to L.A. with a few other guys. There were eight or nine of us staying at a beach house that was just down the walk from the bar scene on Hermosa Pier.

On the day of the event, we went early to the tournament to watch friends roll. Markspray checked his weight, I checked my bracket and then we returned to the beach as our matches weren't until late in the afternoon. Nine Toes was in my group but on the other side of the bracket, which meant I had to win two matches to meet him in the finals. A quiet confidence enveloped me all day, convincing me that this would happen. Maybe this feeling was less about confidence and more about imagery. Maybe the yoga hippies were really onto something, and I was a narrow-minded dick for judging. Hmm....

But as we began the drive from the beach back to the tournament, the butterflies started. I have a technique to stop them which is to keep thinking about the thing that created them in the first place, keep instigating the butterflies until I have no reaction to the original thought that created them, and then they disappear—the damn butterflies vanish, or are supposed to vanish.

Anyway, I was busy with more hippy-yoga-imagery bullshit (see narrow-minded dick above) when a guy on a bike pulled in front of Markspray. He slammed on the brakes. It was a narrow miss.

All of my calm hippy-yoga-imagery flew right out the window, or in layman's terms, I flipped. "Look at this fucker! A fucking helmet! A fucking flashing light! A fucking yellow traffic vest! This fucking guy! He has never known a fucking dangerous moment in his entire fucking pathetic life! He has done everything in his life to ensure absolute FUCKING safety! I AM GOING TO FIGHT NINE TOES RIGHT NOW AND THIS IS WHAT'S IN MY WAY?!" I don't know what happened. Adrenaline? Fear? I don't know, I think that yellow vest put me over-the-top.

Markspray couldn't stop laughing. I stopped screaming but took control of the music. I jammed a CD into the player with the same amount of zeal I had used to scream at that yellow-vested-helmet-wearing biker. "Gonna Fly Now" took over the mood of the car as we proceeded onward. (Yes, guys listen to the theme to *Rocky* all of the time to get pumped up. If there's a better way out there, we have yet to find it.)

Typical to my tournament experiences thus far, the first two matches were not exciting, but I won both. After each match, I returned to the bullpen and waited while watching Nine Toes decimate his opponents. To paraphrase from *The Art of Racing in the Rain*: That which I had manifested was before me. I was to fight him in the finals. My grips were shot, I kneeled on the ground pressing my hand flat and backwards against the hardwood gym floor trying to stretch my forearms. They were so tight and so weak; I don't think I could have tied my own shoes.

Studying Nine Toes during his matches had helped me recognize that he liked to take down his opponents by grabbing their lapels, straight across, one hand on each side, lifting up and giving two quick pops to get his opponent off balance. They'd either end up backwards or over compensate and fall forward. Then he would shove them onto the mat face first. I am guessing he learned this move in football as it resembled a block more than a throw.

While recognizing that I had no throws in my arsenal that would toss Nine Toes, no matter what happened, I would fight for the top. Such a large man probably rarely played guard and I wanted him where I thought he would be mentally weakest. I decided that staying on my feet as long as possible would frustrate and tire the beast.

We high-fived. The match started. Nine Toes went for the lapels and I pushed his hands away. He repeated that strategy. I repeated mine. When he finally seized my lapels he went straight to his big football move. Instead of compensating forward, I allowed him to shove me straight off the mat. His power was more than I had expected. When he lifted me, there were moments where I was on my tippy-toes and then completely off of the mat, running backwards on air. The referee restarted us in the middle. I knew that the ref would allow me to be shoved off the mat one or two more times and then it would cost me a penalty and ultimately disqualification. But, I also knew that even an NFL player gets tired of shoving two hundred and thirty pounds around.

I was shoved off of the mat a second time, no warning from the ref. I could hear Nine Toes breathing heavy. Of course, I was too. When he shoved me to the edge of the mat for the third time, I slid to my right, and then he caught me with his move. I went down. I landed and immediately turtled.* Because he couldn't take my back, he was left with just an advantage point.** I kept my turtle tight as he continued his attempt to take my back.

Surprisingly, I somersaulted into a triangle choke attempt. It was shocking to all involved (me, Nine Toes and every single spectator). The crowd erupted. That's when I first realized that I wasn't the only one fixated on this match. There were six or eight mats with concurrent matches, but our match was the spectators' choice. Unfortunately, Nine Toes was so massive my legs could not get remotely into a choke. He busted the remainder of the attempt wide open. Somersaulting back over, I retreated back into turtle. Then, I felt him over and behind me, and saw his feet on either side of me, and felt his big paw grab the back of my collar. We were separated by a mere thirty-five pounds, but it looked and felt like a hundred and thirty-five with him over me like that.

I immediately knew he would try and pull me backwards to open me up. I also knew he was tired, his grips had to be tired like mine, and he had to be a little worried as I had survived too long. As he pulled

---

* In jiu-jitsu, a turtle is where a competitor is on his knees, elbows in, face into the mat. It sort of resembles bowing to Mecca. A proper turtle makes it difficult to get submissions.
** Advantage points are like partial credit, they don't really count unless the match ends in a tie, then the win goes to the opponent with the most advantage points.

back on my collar full force, I lunged forward. He lost his grip on my collar, fell back and landed on his ass. That's when I spun around into his guard. Success! I was where I had wanted to end up, on top, testing this man's guard.

Megaton and Luka screamed, "Seempson! Forty-five seconds!"

All I had to do was pass his guard in forty-five seconds and I would win. For the first time I saw his face, I could see the concern. That which I manifested was before me. I grabbed his lapels, shoved them into his armpits, and tried to create space to drive my knee into his butt to break him open. As I did, he pulled me down into him, break-ing my posture. Even tired, he was insanely powerful. I restarted the technique.

"Seempson! Thirty Seconds!"

I pressed back and again he broke my posture. Man, was I gassed. This was the finals. I'm up against a tremendous athlete for an oppo-nent. The thought of that became so overpowering that my fatigue broke momentarily into the caverns of my mind. Dread crept in, too. *Fuck that shit. I think I will go ahead and win gold. I may never be here again.* The words to my kids years earlier ran through my mind.

Giving every last effort in my soul, I pressed one final time, I could feel him opening up and then… Time was up.

I had lost.

Or had I? It didn't feel like a loss.

This was one of the greatest moments of my life. I had tested myself, I had not quit, I had strived for greatness. Those six minutes had changed my life. I may have failed, but like Teddy Roosevelt had said, I had "dared greatly." And because of that, "my place shall never be with those cold and timid souls who know neither victory nor defeat."

"It is not the critic who counts; not the man who points out how the strong man stumbles, or where the doer of deeds could have done them better. The credit belongs to the man who is actually in the arena, whose face is marred by dust and sweat and blood, who strives valiantly; who errs and comes short again and again; because there is not effort without error and shortcomings; but who does actually strive to do the deed; who knows the great enthusiasm, the great devotion, who spends himself in a worthy cause, who at the best knows in the end the triumph of high achievement and who at the worst, if he fails, at least he fails while daring greatly. So that his place shall never be with those cold and timid souls who know neither victory nor defeat."

The Man in the Arena
—Theodore Roosevelt

After the medals were dispersed along with accolades from my teammates, I went outside and called Sarah, my ex. It was an impulse move, not a regrettable one, but I was emotional and couldn't quite explain to her adequately what had just happened. When I hung up, I looked around for a moment of solitude, like it would be somewhere outside of me, like it was going to wave me over if we locked eyes. I walked away from the gym and found a quiet patch of grass, then laid flat on my back with the sun in my face and closed my eyes. I visualized where I had been over the previous three years dealing with divorce, all of the training sessions, the good, the bad, Garrett, my uncle, black eyes, new friends, old friends, girlfriends, the ever-chang-ing relationship with my kids…and then I realized that somewhere inside that beautiful mess I had found myself. Crazyland was in the rearview mirror. I was everything that I had always known I could be. That which I had manifested was before me.

Chapter 17

"Every talent must unfold itself in fighting."
—Friedrich Nietzsche

Gotta Light?

On a chilly December night in 2011, in a neighborhood adjacent to Chicago Midway Airport, Anthony Miranda approached a car and asked the occupant for a lighter. The man in the car said he didn't smoke, so Anthony stuck a gun to his head and demanded his wallet, phone and keys instead. The victim explained that he didn't have a wallet and handed the mugger thirty dollars from the car's cup holder. Anthony Miranda backed up and racked the gun, but it jammed, so he racked it a second time freeing the jammed bullet (which fell to the ground). Miranda then picked up the bullet and shouted, "Look, mother fucker, it's a hollow point! I'll blow your brains out!" and then he ordered the occupant out of the car.

At twenty-four years old, Anthony Miranda was already a career criminal. He had been released on probation just a year before this December 2011 night mugging attempt after being convicted in 2007 for residential burglary. He had spent the majority of his adult life

BRUISES   •   81

either committing felonies or serving time for them. Not much scared this guy.

The man Anthony Miranda had at gun point, however, was trained. He was a professional mixed martial arts fighter, and he was former military trained in high-risk hostage rescue. At present he worked part-time in close protection security.

Miranda kept the pistol pointed at the man's chest but that made little difference. In a flash his trained victim redirected the gun causing Miranda to shoot his own ankle before being taken down.

"I wasn't scared because I am trained," explained the man who asked to remain anonymous.

After the take down, the anonymous trained victim gave Miranda two black eyes and multiple lacerations about his face. In short, he looked like he had been tossed through the windshield.

During the scuffle, Anthony Miranda initially fought back, but ultimately begged for his own freedom, crying and begging and explaining that he had a baby.[21]

The victim did not release him, but instead chose to contain the villain until police arrived. Then he quietly left the scene refusing to allow reporters to capture any part of him on film or digitally. He walked off leaving them without so much as a picture of any part of him, not his hands, not his torso, and certainly not his face.

Chapter 18

"*Our life is what our thoughts make it.*"
—Marcus Aurelius
Roman Emperor and Philosopher

Hawaii

AFTER THE PAN AMS, A TRIP TO HAWAII WITH MY FRIEND GREG WAS IN order. The two of us landed on the Big Island and stayed at his time share in Kona. Being two single guys, we found Kona to be a little bit sleepy and decided to head to Honolulu. But before we left I wanted to do two things:

- See Kilauea and its lava up close & personal.
- Scuba dive some of the old lava tubes around the island.

Jiu-jitsu was helping me understand that life is about adventure, not just the party.

We drove to Kilauea to get our up close & personal experience with the Ring of Fire. We stood in front of the park ranger at the Volcanoes National Park Visitor Center in running shoes, T-shirts and shorts. He gave us the once-over and sternly proclaimed that we were not prepared to hike to see the lava. We apparently needed jeans, leather gloves, sturdy shoes, a gallon of water each and two flash lights with extra batteries. We swung into the gift shop, bought two flash-lights, four bottles of water and some salted sunflower seeds, then jumped back into the jeep and headed to the trailhead anyway. See that? We only partially ignored his advice. I'm evolving by the second.

About an hour later, we finally arrived at the trailhead, which is where the road ends abruptly because recent lava flows had reclaimed it as Kilauea's. We loaded up the backpack with our supplies. At the trailhead there was another ranger who was proudly standing next to her telescope, which was pointed at an orange lava creek way off in the distance. She excitedly asked us if we'd like to view the lava.

"Nah, we're going to look at it up close." I stated plainly, visibly crushing her spirit. Apparently orange lava creeks are pretty cool and worth gazing at through a telescope. They're rare.

She, too, declared us unfit for the journey. With nothing better to do at that point, we took a peek at the creek, and then we oohed and ahhed a bit. Our reaction was affected, but it must have also been charming because she handed over the directions to the lava.

For as far as we could see, the two thousand degree molten rock had burned every last piece of vegetation off of the island's surface and replaced it with pillow-shaped, brittle, razor sharp hardened basaltic rock. The undulating black rock was shaped more like short sand dunes which was in significant contrast to the angular weathered volcanic rock of Arizona.

As we looked toward the trail head, the ocean was to our right and the banks of the shield volcano were to our left. Way off in the distance on our left was an orange creek of molten lava. And to the right of that was steam rising up from where the base of a cliff met the ocean. The lava was clearly in the process of adding real estate.

The directions were fairly simple, walk one-half mile along the last of the remaining road to the trail head, look out across the moonscaped earth as far to the horizon as we could see and find a blinking yellow beacon (which really was a traffic barricade). Then, walk to that beacon and then scan the horizon for the next beacon and walk to that. The guide suggested that we repeat this exercise fourteen times. Once we reached the fourteenth beacon, we were supposed to walk toward ten o'clock for forty-five minutes, at which point we would be at the lava.

Greg and I began the journey. We were pretty excited and flying past traffic barricades quickly and without much thought. Our abrupt actions were bordering on mocking all the warnings we had received and ignored. The ocean breeze was coming in from the direction we were headed in—paralleling the shoreline—and it felt good as it cooled us on the hike. Sharp rock crunched under our feet as we plodded along while joking and eating our salted sunflower seeds. At barricade fourteen, using our engineering and survey skills, we strategically lined up our ten o'clock route, marked the time on my watch and then proceeded to embark on the last forty-five minutes of the hike.

After forty-five minutes on the nose, we stopped and looked around. We could not find the lava as promised. To our left, one mile up on the slope, was the orange creek. As we turned to face the lava, we could see that steam was rising from the ocean about one mile behind us. Greg was busy video recording our adventure, so I made an executive decision that we should head toward the lava on the slope. And so we headed directly up the slope. Five minutes into this decision my mind caught up with where we were. We were standing directly on top of two thousand degree lava that had burrowed into the crusty surface and tunneled to the sea where the steam was rising. I didn't know how far below the surface this lava was residing, but it was there, under us somewhere. As this thought pulsated in my mind, the wind changed direction and it suddenly felt like an oven door had just opened, or, more accurately, like The Gates of Hell had. I looked at Greg for reassurance, but he was covered in sweat and dripping everywhere as he tied his sopping wet shirt around his head. Looking at Greg was a really bad idea. The wind blew steadily from the top of the hill across the molten lava and into our faces. Greg asked me for some water out of the backpack. The heat, the sweat, the five mile hike and the salty sunflower seeds had finally coaxed our thirst into surfacing. I reached into the backpack and found one. I didn't find two or three or four water bottles, I found only one water bottle. This meant, to get engineering precise, that there were 16.9 ounces (just over two cups) of water for both of us. Those rangers may have been onto something....

As we looked back on five miles, ninety minutes and thirty-five degrees cooler ago, we realized there was what one might dub as a "miscommunication" about packing the water. To this day, I blame Greg, and conversely he blames me. And, mostly, we try not to bring it up. At any rate, we started rationing. This didn't deter us, mind you—we figured if we rationed the water and ditched the sunflower seeds we'd be good to go—and so we forged onward. To the lava we went!

Suddenly, the heat was almost too much, but the orange lava creek was still the better part of four hundred yards up the slope. As I squinted towards the destination through the waves of heat rising off of the surface, I noticed some black rock moving as if a gofer was blazing a trail from it to us. No such thing as a molten rock gofer! The molten rock had cooled, turning it from orange to black, and it had coagulated slightly, but was still plenty hot and was blocking the path to the orange creek. The sight was unnerving. And this was happening about fifty yards in front of us. If I hadn't noticed the movement, it would have been invisible. We decided that this was as close as we were going to get, on this day anyway.

After taking some time to gulp down the last bit of water and shoot some pictures, it was time to head back. Since there was no official trail, we opted to take a more direct route back. Instead of walking back toward the ocean and making a right, we decided to cut straight out along the hypotenuse to complete our triangle back to the car.

Within ten steps of this new route, I felt a burst of hot air shoot straight up my shorts. Well, at least my balls were now dry. Of course, there was no time to enjoy that comforting sensation because as I looked down I noticed the soles of my shoes were melting, creating a sliding effect with every step. Greg must have felt the heat because we both began sprinting with our knees up like we were doing high school football tire drills. After twenty-five yards, our shoes stopped melting and the overall temperature cooled. We stopped, looked wide-eyed at each other and started giggling the giggle that only near-death experiences can bring on. We finished by logically retracing our path back to the car where three bottles of water awaited us.

The next day was our scuba adventure. I am certified, Greg was not. The dive company was going to "resort certify" him while I went to see the lava tubes.

That morning, Greg and I were greeted at the dock by our dive master and her crew. Plainly put, our dive master was hot. The crew took us out about forty-five minutes from the dock where they informed Greg that the hot dive master would take him out by the anchor line to make sure he had some basic scuba skills, such as the know-how to clear his mask. After that, she would "resort certify" him and then he could dive that day with us under her team's direct supervision. While they went through this, the other instructor and I would dive to find some of the lava tubes and chase a few sea turtles around. The idea was that Greg and the dive master would meet up with us during my tour.

They never showed.

After thirty or forty minutes of seeing the underwater sites, we returned to the boat.

I crawled onto the metal dive boat to find Greg relaxed and flirting it up with the hot dive master. Apparently, Greg geared up and swam out to the anchor line as planned. But when the hot dive master instructed Greg to follow her down the anchor line where he was to complete a series of basic scuba diving skills, he froze up. About thirty seconds in, claustrophobia set in and Greg darted for the surface in a panic. Greg tapped out.

What I love about Greg is that when it comes to the ladies, he has no shame. Where most men would have quietly retreated away from the embarrassment (the hot dive master), Greg charged forward and opted to charm his way back into her good graces. I approached just as they were discussing the specific situation that had caused Greg to throw in the towel on an amateur scuba diving career.

"So, how deep were we? It felt pretty deep, I mean I could feel the pressure on my ears. What was it, like, twenty feet?" Greg asked confidently as if he had just set some sort of record.

"Four," she retorted. "You were four feet deep."

With that, Greg and I burst out laughing hysterically.

Mocking himself Greg blurted out, "Help me! I'm drowning!"

Dryly, I replied, "Greg, it's four feet deep, just stand up."

With that, the entire boat joined us in our fit of laughter. The great thing about Greg is that he doesn't mind being the source of everyone's entertainment, which is fortunate for him because after years of friendship he often was our main source of mockery. And it has never interfered whatsoever when it came to him picking up girls, which was impressive, truly impressive. Frequently, it worked to his advantage. In fact, we met up with our hot dive guide that night for some drinks.

The following day, we headed to Honolulu.

After two more days in Waikiki we were spent. Greg asked me what my plan was for our last day. My plan was simple, it was to eat some breakfast and spend the day drinking at Duke's until the sun went down or I passed out. Duke's is a tourist bar on the beach. Greg decided that it was a fine plan and joined me. We added one general guideline to the plan: no buying drinks for girls. Any girl we met would have to be without the crutch. Well, either they'd be without the crutch or we would. I guess it depends how you look at that. Huh? Anyway....

It was a splendid day, and one where Greg just seemed to get funnier as the afternoon progressed. We did meet some girls. He did eventually offend their better sensibilities. And they did storm off, but only to return. That happened several times with several gaggles of gals. This pattern had me laughing until my face actually hurt.

The Canadian tourist sitting next to us was laughing at his antics, too. He eventually struck up a conversation and asked me about my T-shirt. (I was wearing my 2007 Pan American Tournament shirt.) I began to explain jiu-jitsu. He was in his early thirties and he used to be a professional boxer. It was friendly bar conversation. We began to further discuss the two combat sports. He didn't accept that I could effectively get him to the ground and keep him there from jiu-jitsu training alone. I asked if he would like to go down to the beach and have a fight to prove it. He thought I was crazy. There was no anger or bravado in my request. I was actually curious to know if I could "kill" a professional boxer. I did put in a request that if he knocked me out, he would also help me come to, and I promised to do the same for him. He declined the fight, but not a drink. So we continued drinking as the conversation turned into your basic bar banter. We talked about chicks and made fun of Greg.

It was well into the evening, the sun had long set and no one had passed out, but it was time to go, nonetheless. I asked for the check. Aside from the lunches we had bought, the three hundred dollar tab looked more like a scroll with the word *beer* repeatedly typed down it. I closed one eye to alleviate my double vision and looked it over:

1 Beer @ $3.75

1 Beer @ $3.75

2 Island Burgers @ $7.95

1 Beer @ $3.75

1 Beer @ $3.75

1 Beer @ $3.75

1 Beer @ $3.75

1 Beer @ $3.75

1 Beer @ $3.75

1 Beer @ $3.75

1 Beer @ $3.75

1 Beer @ $3.75

1 Beer @ $3.75

1 Beer @ $3.75

1 Beer @ $3.75

1 Beer @ $3.75

1 Beer @ $3.75

1 Beer @ $3.75

1 Beer @ $3.75

1 Beer @ $3.75

1 Beer @ $3.75

1 Beer @ $3.75

1 Beer @ $3.75

1 Beer @ $3.75

1 Beer @ $3.75

1 Beer @ $3.75

1 Beer @ $3.75

1 Beer @ $3.75

1 Beer @ $3.75

1 Beer @ $3.75

1 BeEr @ $3.75

1 Beer @ $3.75

1 Beer @ $3.75

1 Beer @ $3.75

1 Beer @ $3.75

1 Beer @ $3.75

1 Beer @ $3.75

1 Beer @ $3.75

1 Beer @ $3.75

1 Beer @ $3.75

1 Beer @ $3.75

1 Beer @ $3.75

1 Beer @ $3.75

1 Beer @ $3.75

1 Beer @ $3.75

1 Beer @ $3.75

1 Beer @ $3.75

1 Beer @ $3.75

1 Beer @ $3.75

1 Beer @ $3.75

1 Beer @ $3.75

1 Beer @ $3.75

1 Beer @ $3.75

1 Beer @ $3.75

1 Beer @ $3.75

1 Beer @ $3.75

1 Beer @ $3.75

1 Beer @ $3.75

1 Beer @ $3.75

1 Beer @ $3.75

1 Beer @ $3.75

1 Mudslide @ $10.25

1 Beer @ $3.75

1 Beer @ $3.75

1 Beer @ $3.75

Greg broke the rule.

Chapter 19

"Fatigue makes cowards of us all."
—George Patton and Vince Lombardi

The Tournament Bug

IN 2007, AFTER MY UPLIFTING LOSS TO NINE TOES, I WAS ON FIRE AND went on a jiu-jitsu tournament spree. In addition to the Pan Americans, I competed in the Arizona Open, Arizona State Championships, The Worlds, and the American Nationals. The tournament after the Pan Americans was the Arizona State Championships. I felt confident-based on my performance in the Pan Americans—that I would take gold in my division, although nothing is ever guaranteed.

The day was fantastic; all my friends were there competing. My first match was against a guy I had met twice before, once beating him as a white belt and once losing to him as a blue belt (just three months earlier). He had tossed me pretty good in that loss. You know it's a hard takedown when you hit the mat and hear the crowd groan. But on this fine day, I beat him, which led me into my second match.

My second match was with an opponent who was about 6'5" and

close to three hundred pounds, but he didn't have a Jarrod Bunch physique (Nine Toes). This guy looked like he had never skipped a meal or dessert since birth. I knew that I didn't want to get stuck under him, so I decided that it'd be best to fight hard for top position. He was accommodating and pulled guard. Then he surprised me by using my very own bread and butter sweep (known as a Flower Sweep). I went over like a felled tree and was mounted. He grape-vined my legs and drove his belly into my abdomen—pushing all the air out of my lungs. I must have looked like a mechanic stuck under a VW Bug—nothing but arms and legs showing. I even got a face full of man boobs that, in spite of the sweep's name, did not smell like flowers. I could not breathe. I tapped. After that, I had a final match for third place. I won that match and took the bronze. The really cool part about this event was looking across the mats and seeing Aaron competing on one and Greg competing on another.

After my consecutive defeats to Nine Toes and VW Bug, I decided it was time to drop a few pounds. I had quit smoking in January and could feel my cardiovascular capacities increase. My mind and body were morphing some more. Dropping fifteen to twenty pounds would put me into a bracket that would be more size appropriate and limit the size of my opponent to two hundred and twenty-one pounds. Also, I liked the thought of matches that looked more like jiu-jitsu and less like two bears fighting over a salmon. Basically, I wanted out of Fat Ass Division so badly, that I had decided to take drastic measures to cut the weight. It was June and the World Jiu-jitsu Championships were in August.

I started out at 233 pounds, which was fit for me. My body was comfortable at that weight. They say that losing the last five is always a real bitch-well, I knew that my last five actually meant twelve. Plus, they weigh us at tournaments with our gi on, so I had to allot for that. Let's call it my last fifteen pounds, to be safe. So, my final fifteen, every single pound of it, was going to take focus. Summer in Phoenix helped a little—it's too fucking hot to eat here, so at least I had that on my side. And a ten minute trip anywhere in a car—where the interior was holding steady around 150 —could shed a pound in a pinch. I was hopeful about this plan, not cocky, just optimistic.

Well, after one month of intensive cardio vascular training combined with a healthier diet, less alcohol, and upping the intensity and frequency of jiu-jitsu practice, I weighed in at 231 pounds. Yep! Two whole pounds! I know, I know, I should have written a book on weight loss. Now, I had about a month to drop twelve more pounds. It was time to get seriously serious. Again. And so I did. I began running three miles twice a day in a hoodie. Yes, in Phoenix. Yes, in the summer. I cut my calories down to twelve hundred per day. I actually counted my fucking calories. Aaron started calling me Jenny Craig. I continued training jiu-jitsu three times per week. I was miserable. I had no energy for the mat, people were crushing me. I did lose weight, though, almost four pounds per week.

Three weeks and ten pounds into that torturous adventure, I decided to renew my membership on an online dating site. I think wearing hoodies in the summer in Phoenix must have been frying my brain because normally when guys are in training mode they're also not in girl mode. (Although, part of me always seems to be "on" when it comes to women; it's a blessing and a curse.) I was definitely hungry (for food) when I wrote that ad, though. They say that there are four states of existence that can lead an alcoholic to drink, especially when combined. Those states are hungry, angry, lonely, tired. It's called: HALT. And, you're supposed to halt when that happens and reassess your next move. I was all of those: hungry, angry, lonely, tired. I wonder if there's a ton of other things you shouldn't be doing when you're hungry, angry, lonely and tired besides not having a drink? Like say, rewrite your online dating profile.

After numerous weird and goofy online dates, I have decided that I should be more honest with my approach:

First, looks matter to me. I am shallow in this area. I would like someone who is less than 135 pounds. This rule is not written in stone. For example, say you are tall or you have a big chest, I am not a pig, there are exceptions. By the way, chest size does not matter to me.

Height: Anything over 5 feet. I am 6'3." Ideally, I really like girls over 5' 8." If you are over 5' 10," well that is just hot.

I am not into BBW. If you have ever described yourself as BBW do not respond. This means you are fat and I am not into fat.

Personality: I like happy, optimistic people. So, my personality requirements are simple: Don't be a bitch.

I would like someone who is 21-to-35 years old. I put the floor at 21 because I like to go to the bar and have a few drinks. If you have a good fake ID, I will go as low as 18. But, while the 18-to-24 age group tends to be hot chicks, they also know it and therefore are uninterest-

ing because they don't feel like they have to work for it. As such, I put my age "sweet spot" between 27 and 33. This group is still hot, but has learned to kick in some INTERESTING personality because they know the clock is ticking.

If you like "clubbing" I am not for you. I said bars, not clubs.

Hair color: I am flexible in this category, any color, except grey. Also, I tend to prefer brunettes as they seem to age better.

Next item: kids. I am fine with you having kids, I just don't want to meet them. I have kids, but you are not going to meet them. This does not mean that I am not into you. It means that I don't split my kids' time with others. You shouldn't either. This will not change.

If you have ever posted a picture of yourself with your kids on a dating site, DEFINITELY DO NOT RESPOND. When I see women posting a picture of themselves with their kids, it always freaks me out. It may as well be an ad to acquire a child molester.

If you have ever posted a picture of your pet on a dating site, it is not a deal breaker, but just know that I am not into dating animals. I am trying to date you, not your little dog, Scruffy.

If you are looking for The One, you should know I am not it. Don't get me wrong, I would love to hug a hobbit or ride a unicorn, I just don't see it happening.

Lastly; look like your picture. If we decide to meet and you look like you ate the girl in the picture, or you look like the mother of the girl in the picture, I am walking. All my pictures are less than two years old; it's only fair that your pictures be current.

So, with THAT dating ad, I met a girl online the very next day. We had scheduled to meet for a drink after work on a Thursday at a restaurant in Scottsdale. I had a meeting for the design of a round-about in Safford, Arizona that day. Safford is about a six hour round trip drive from Phoenix. The business trip was timed so that I could swing by my place and get cleaned up before meeting her. But on the drive back, my lack of calories and heavy workouts—coupled with a long straight boring road—caught up with me. I pulled over to take a nap on the side of the highway. When I woke up, I was drenched in sweat and had eaten up all my extra time. Heading straight to the date was my only option. And I didn't feel like I had the luxury to be late, even if I called. I mean, after THAT dating ad, it seemed to me that I had used up all of my get-out-of-jail-free cards, at least for the first date.

The restaurant was next to the Scottsdale Fashion Mall. I darted into Dillard's, cleaned up in their restroom, went out to the display area and took a quick sample cologne bath.

My date arrived looking just like her pictures. She was Asian and absolutely beautiful. She had been recently separated, which led me to believe she resided somewhere in Crazyland, but maybe just the burbs because she came off intelligent and interesting, and she seemed relaxed. And she either didn't notice my disheveled appearance, or was too polite to comment. After drinks, we decided to get dinner. Given the level of fatigue I was experiencing, I decided to indulge in a piece of salmon.

What did I say about the four states of existence that can lead an alcoholic to drink? Well, that salmon was the gateway drug to my downfall. Maybe it was the salmon talking, but the conversation seemed incredible, and the girl was gorgeous, and I needed a drink. Six margaritas did the trick. She had a sweet tooth, we ordered the tiramisu. It was glorious! So glorious was that damned tiramisu that we stopped at Cold Stone Creamery for an ice cream topper.

Thanks to my dick doing the thinking for me once again and that goddamned tiramisu, I was headed across the Arizona desert with my heater and seat warmers on in the middle of August for the World Jiu-jitsu Championships in Long Beach, California. You know you have reached freak status when truckers in the Quick Stop bathroom are looking at you strangely while you're standing on the quarter operat-ed scale in a full sweat suit and it's 118 degrees outside. It worked; the last three pounds were successfully sweated out of me. I was just below weight when I arrived at the hotel that night. Hungry and exhausted, I chose sleep to get my mind off of food.

The next morning was the first time in my life that I had ever eaten breakfast naked, while standing on a scale and holding my gi. The hotel bathroom scale had me at 218 pounds. I picked up the banana off of the counter and was still under 221 pounds. Then I picked up a yogurt, still good. Then I snatched up the bottle of water. Over weight! Crap! I poured out some water. At weight! Indulge!

Worlds has no age brackets, so I was in with the young guys. But at thirty-eight, I still felt like I could hold my own against them. I was the first match on the mats that morning. I would love to tell you a ter-rific story of excellence, but God only gives me those on rare occa-sions, when I need them most. I went for an uchi mata, which is a type of hip throw, but I didn't commit to it, so my opponent landed on me in side control. I spent the remaining time trying to escape and lost. But I felt like a winner anyway. Megaton and Luka had both come to coach and watch my match. I didn't medal, but I did find the nearest In-N-Out Burger and awarded myself a cheeseburger for the first time all summer. Like the tiramisu weeks before, it was fucking glorious.

Two months later I followed up with another less than stellar performance at the American Nationals, and with that the 2007 tournament season was over for me.

Noteworthy? No. But, I was twenty pounds lighter and an official nonsmoker—not a total loss after all. And I was on my way to having a girlfriend, or as close to having one as I had been in a long, long while (Girlfriend ✓).

Chapter 20

"This is your life and it's ending one minute at a time."
—*Fight Club*
By Chuck Palahniuk

The Purple People Eater

IT WAS CHRISTMAS TIME IN 2007, WHICH MEANT IT WAS BELT PROMOTION season. Given the two years at blue belt, the heavy tournament season I had just endured, and the fact that I was beating every other blue belt in class, I was hoping to receive my purple belt at the party. But before that fine celebration, I had to plan my own company's Christmas party.

That year I took the office to a privately rented space at Dave & Buster's for the company Christmas Party. In case you live in a well-insulated box at the North Pole, Dave & Buster's is a bar/arcade/bowling alley, or your average adult playground. Business was good; it was a time to be happy. I handed out bonuses and we had a White Elephant exchange. Although times were good, I could sense a change in the economy. I just didn't understand it yet, but I was receiving a definite hippy vibe about the foreshadowing of shitty economic times to come. However, I truly believed that this group of people and I would be able to ride out the storm in our little corporate boat.

We left the rented room and went out into Dave & Buster's and bowled, played pool and other various games. I walked up on a couple of my guys playing the mini-basketball machine. They had been challenged by two cocky assholes. It wasn't the challenge that made these two assholes assholes, it was the fact that they were assholes that made them assholes. They made a nominal wager with my employees, Keith and Greg, and they kept jaw-jabbering right up until they lost. I began chiding them as they had done to my friends throughout the entire game. The louder of the two assholes didn't like what I was saying and puffed up.

This moment would normally have gotten my adrenaline pumping, I might have become slightly shaky. I would have mirrored and puffed up as well. But I didn't. As I leaned against the wall, he got in my space and very loudly made some disparaging comment about my vagina and my lack of basketball skills. I took a monk pose, which is a non-threatening way demonstrated by Renzo Gracie to get your hands up to fend off the cheap shot. Very calmly I said, "Basketball isn't my game anymore, but I will bet you that I can choke you out in less than sixty seconds."

I was provoking the bigger asshole, and it was out of character for me. Maybe my economic worries were bubbling up and beginning to manifest in weird places. A new form of Crazyland? At any rate, this comment pushed the bigger asshole over the edge. He shoved me. My hands were up, I deflected and laughed. Then, his friend jumped in front of him. Security/high school bowling alley employees moved toward us. Not wanting to get arrested, I told him that if he was really feeling it, he should come to Megaton Jiu-jitsu the following morning and I would be there. He, too, noticed the security/high school bowling alley employees and moved on. The Christmas party resumed as usual and wound down at some bar in Scottsdale around 2:00 A.M.

I arrived at Megaton's the next morning. While using a wall as leverage to appear relaxed and cool—but to actually steady myself cause I was hung over as hell—I told Megaton about the previous night and the surprise visitors we might get. Although, most of me knew that Little Barking Dog wouldn't show up, I had to show my face, just in case. Megaton had simply responded, "That's why we are here, Seempson."

I think the asshole got the last laugh. I mean, I only came to practice on the off-chance that he might, but then I had to stay and train with a gigantic hangover. I could have kicked the crap out of the asshole while hung over, but my sparring partners were another story for they took full advantage of my state that morning. It wasn't pretty. It was at that point that I realized that I was truly ready for jiu-jitsu to kick my ego permanently into oblivion.

A week later it was time for the jiu-jitsu Christmas party. The party was at a Mexican joint owned by Markspray's ex-wife. Aaron received his blue belt. I did not receive my purple belt. I was really happy for Aaron, but extremely disappointed about not getting a promotion to purple.

You tell yourself that these belts don't mean anything, that the truth is on the mat, but they do mean something. They symbolize effort, achievement and recognition. When people who train ask you your belt rank or see your belt rank, it means something to them.

Years later, when I received my brown belt, Professor Ellwanger put it like this (I am paraphrasing):

A white belt generally has no poison, but blue belts are tricky, some have poison and others don't. You have to play with the blue belt to see. You know a purple has poison, but a purple belt may have just a few ways of delivering it. The brown and the black belts have poison and a multitude of ways of delivering it.

I wanted to be the guy with poison. I felt that all of my efforts, tournaments, training, improvements—watching guys I regularly tapped out get their purple belts—felt futile. It was unfair. So, yeah, it mattered.

I had won a bottle of whiskey at the jiu-jitsu party. It wasn't a purple belt, but it was free booze. Aaron and I drank it as our designated driver took us to the next party. Between that bottle and the mass of beverages we consumed at the second party, we were pretty sloppy. This made the drive home extra interesting for Aaron and our DD, as I pontificated rather boisterously about my missing purple belt and how all the other "real" purple belts were about to feel my wrath. I was going to become a Purple People Eater!

And that's exactly what I did, sort of. I spent much of January choosing the purple belts to roll with and trying to roll in front of

Megaton to show him that I was worthy. All that arrogance on my part was imperfect. It was not Zen and I was no better than the loud mouth drunk at the end of the bar yelling for the sake of attention. I was the bigger of the two assholes. It was official. Maybe a belt promotion is not just about your performance on the mat, maybe it's about your overall performance in life.

Thinking back on that time, I realized that my behavior was kind of sad, or pathetic. I'm talking about the mood I was bringing into the dojo. I mean two guys start to roll, but one is on the hunt and the other doesn't know it. Well, that's sort of an ambush. And the mere fact that I had this attitude probably was a good indicator that I was not ready to be a purple belt. Even thirty-eight year olds can be childish. Again, this was a new form of Crazyland. The second part of my plan was to begin another year of tournaments, this time starting in Europe!

Purple belt or not, Europe was going to meet "Seempson." Now this was probably a good indicator that I was going to be ready for a belt promotion real soon.

Chapter 21

"It snowed last year too:
I made a snowman and my brother knocked it down
And I knocked my brother down
And then we had tea."
—Dylan Thomas

Brothers

AARON HAS THREE BROTHERS AND HE IS THE THIRD YOUNGEST. ONE NIGHT I was invited to his youngest brother, Daryl's, for a house warming party. Also in attendance was his second oldest brother, Byron.

Daryl's house was quite a drive from my house, bordering on an hour away. Remember, 2008 was just at the end of the housing bubble and the saying in Phoenix was, "drive until you qualify." Daryl had done exactly that. Aaron, Daryl, Byron and I had gotten pretty drunk on a number of occasions over the years. They are of Scottish heritage; they're yuppies who can pound the drinks with ease. I could tell that this was heading down the same path. I kept my drinking to a minimum and began to make my exit before I wouldn't be able to make the long drive home. But Aaron couldn't let me just leave. He began to chide his brothers with my jiu-jitsu prowess. He had already choked his brothers out on other drunken backyard grappling adventures, but these two would not accept that I could catch them. We went to the back yard (which in Arizona means that we were ankle deep in gravel).

First I choked out Daryl, then Byron, and then back to Daryl and then back to Byron. Aaron drank and laughed at his brothers on the sidelines until they called him out and he took my place. The pattern repeated itself. Finally, they gave up on both Aaron and me and went after each other. We became spectators. This is where Aaron and I coined the term, "like two bears fighting over a salmon." They were burley guys, slapping each other around. It looked so sloppy and futile…like two bears fighting over a salmon.

Aaron wasn't the only one excited about getting his brothers back with his new found talent. When I came into this world, my brother made it his personal goal to send me back. Glenn is three and a half years older than me, so growing up he was always much bigger. I spent ages zero-to-fifteen in survival mode. I never knew where the attack would come from or what would spark it. I just knew it usually ended with my brother mounted on me dripping his spit as close to my face as he could before sucking it back into his mouth. It's like, one day he woke up, sat in bed and thought, "What should I do today? Oh, I know, I will see how many times I can punch Mike." And that is what the sadistic douche did for the rest of our lives together under our parent's roof.

To this day, if I am in a pool with Glenn, I keep one eye on him. More than once my parents had to come to my rescue because Glenn was drowning me-not sort of drowning me, actually drowning me. If he was a child today, he would be a prime candidate for Ritalin. What's funny about all of this was that my parents never seemed to come to my rescue until I was seconds from death; it was like they just didn't seem to notice unless I was bleeding or not breathing.

When I was six, Glenn was attacking me cause he woke up and decided to, and I was screaming. Our parents became so frustrated with the noise that they had decided it was time to settle this once and for all. Their idea was to have Glenn and I fight in the kitchen while they watched—no rules, no referee—just a fight to the finish, AND THEY WERE PUBLIC SCHOOL TEACHERS! Actually, by that time my dad was a principal and my mom was back in college working on her Master's degree in English. I don't know what stopped them from selling tickets! Honestly, the only thing missing from their parenting style, or lack thereof, was that they didn't commercialize their bohemian tactics and profit from them. I shouldn't belittle my parents. They were loving parents and they had their collective hands full with Glenn.

I am pretty sure I don't have to explain how the fight went. What is even more shocking is that this throw-down in the kitchen, or as I like to call it, "The Twitchin in the Kitchen Incident of 1974" (based on the movements of my remains after I was left on the floor in the fetal position), did not settle it once and for all. I mean it did for me, although dominance was never a question in my mind. And I think my parents felt a special, unbiased, unequivocal resolution. I mean, Glenn had won the not-so-fair-and-square fight. They could now shut the door forever on our sibling discourse. Glenn was the winner. And

I thought that at least they had witnessed firsthand how lopsided these fights were, and that everyone could now move on with their lives. He successfully beat me, with full parental permission, into a balled-up mass of sweat, tears and fears. I was bloodied, bruised and don't get me started on the emotional effects of it all. But Glenn apparently felt that there was still more to be proven. And so for years to come I would dutifully play the role of punching bag to my brother and to most of his buddies. Now, I did get my licks in, but only after I had been pushed to the brink and only in sneak-attack form. I was a "shover" more than a puncher. I remember one time my brother had finished his beat-down on me and got up to leave. When he turned, I sprung up, hit him in the back with everything I had. His shoulder blades turning into book ends from the impact of my fist, and before he could react, I shoved him down a flight of stairs. He tumbled all the way down. I am smiling now as I think about this momentary victory. And even though I heard him crying as he hit the landing, I couldn't tell you how he must have looked—all crumpled up at the bottom of the stairs—because I didn't stick around to bask in the moment. I hauled ass out of the house as fast as my skinny legs took me!

That summer we took a family road trip from California to Florida. Like most little kids, I was into caves and dinosaurs and wanted to see Carlsbad Cavern in New Mexico. It was the only tourist stop on the entire trip that I wanted to see. During the tour, Glenn continued the torment. He couldn't give me an hour to enjoy the place. I finally shoved him, nearly into the Bottomless Pit. My parents were pissed. One shove back to his one hundred and fifty and I'm the bad guy?! Alright, fine, it was toward the Bottomless Pit, but it's not like he would have died. It was a bottomless pit; he would still be falling today. As a tortured little brother, the idea of Glenn falling forever and ever was genuinely pleasing.

When we got older, he took up wrestling and football and I took up soccer and basketball. Although, I did play two years of high school football, I just wasn't the aggressive type, it wasn't really my sport. I always swore one day that I'd be bigger than Glenn and get my revenge. But I didn't outgrow him until college, and by then he had police academy training under his belt to supplement his wrestling. I could hold my own at that point, but still wasn't able to dominate him. Was this ever going to end? By the time college was over, I had conceded to the notion that I would never be able to fully kick Glenn's ass.

Eventually, twenty years passed. It seemed I was going to be Glenn's bitch for life. And then along came jiu-jitsu. One Thanksgiving, during my time as a blue belt, we were at my dad's house. Maybe it was the feel of the old place, who knows, but Glenn fired a look at me like he might attack.

I smiled and said, "Glenn, you look froggy. I'll put you right there on the floor and work you over and there is not a goddamned thing you will be able to do about it. You care to try?"

The look in his eyes was hard to describe, they got beady; there was fire. He's had this look since childhood, and I knew it well. Maybe I had over-sold my offer, maybe discretion was the better part of valor, and maybe it was time to shelf our childhood antics forever. Whatever it was, he knew I had been doing jiu-jitsu and the fire went out of his eyes. He did not take me up on the fight.

Several months later, his wife signed him up for jiu-jitsu as a Christmas present. Several months after that, Glenn came to train at Megaton's while on a visit to Phoenix. The day I had been waiting for had arrived. We began to roll. I worked him over, but he was having problems with his back, so it didn't count. I went to visit him and we went to train at his school in California. The instructor put the brothers in the middle and the rest of the class circled up to watch the sibling rivalry. It was a no gi match. He started well, but I finished better. I don't remember the particulars of the match, just that I dominated, and at the end there was no feeling of vindication. As a matter of fact, it was underwhelming. He wasn't an asshole anymore. I actually loved my big brother. (That sentence is probably an indication of Stockholm syndrome.) My jiu-jitsu was so far in front of his that there was no doubt about the outcome. Maybe I should have taken mount and dripped spit in his face only to suck it back in, or did the big brother xylophone on his ribs, or tickled under his chin until he peed his gi, or made him hit himself until he cried, or punched him in the shoulder until he said "uncle."

But I didn't. I just tapped him out and, I suppose, fulfilled a promise to the ten year old version of myself that one day that vengeance would be mine. All those years as a kid waiting for the moment and when it arrived, it meant almost nothing.

That is irony.

Chapter 22

"Bullfight critics ranked in rows
Crowd the enormous Plaza full;
But there is only one who knows-
And he's the one who fights the bull."
—Domingo Ortega
Matador

2008 European Championships

My 2008 jiu-jitsu season began with a trip to Portugal for the European Championships. I was still irked about not getting the promotion to purple belt and was determined to show Megaton that he had missed something. The tournament was in late January.

My plane landed in London. I caught a connection to Lisbon where I met up with Megaton. The hotel was across the street from a bullfighting arena. Seeing the ring reminded me of the Domingo Ortega bullfighting poem that John Kennedy used to carry around in his pocket. In a way, martial arts is like bullfighting. It's just you against the bull. And most of the time, the bull is yourself, not your opponent. There were some Megaton affiliate school athletes there as well, but I was the only student from Phoenix. After the long flight and below par airport food, I was unsure of my weight. But the nice thing about this tournament was that the open weight division was before the weighted divisions. That meant that I'd get a match or three in where weight did not matter. I knew that this would help knock off the jet lag plus jumpstart my system if I needed to shed a couple of pounds, so I entered.

My first opponent was a British guy who weighed about 190 pounds. He pulled guard, but I partially passed and we crashed to the ground. I had his leg trapped, and in that moment, a move I had learned from Royler Gracie came to me. To visualize the trap, think of a person sitting Indian style. If you lay on top of the legs and control the leg on top, the leg underneath has nowhere to go and is therefore locked in place. I had trapped his legs in such a manner, and then began to slide around to side control. As I executed it, Megaton yelled, *"Good Seempson, good. Now pass!"*

I did. The points were mine. I really wanted to finish this opponent, so I probably overplayed my position late in the match. And as a result of that, he had recovered guard and I got complacent. He dropped a triangle choke on me. *If you can breathe, you can fight, and you can breathe so you can fight.* I freed my arm and made a posture correction which made the triangle more difficult to execute (and also so I could breathe.) *Did you really fly all the way over here to NOT bring back a souvenir???* With my posture up—imagine a man praying on his knees and looking to God; now lose the halo and that's me—I grabbed the leg and pealed it off, freeing myself from the danger as time expired. I won the match. Megaton had witnessed it, and I was hoping that my prowess had proved that I was worthy of a promotion to purple.

The next match was against a man from Switzerland who was exactly my size—same height and weight to the kilo. I pulled guard and he passed and then held tight. He did what I should have done in the previous match. It was boring, but enough for him to get the win. However, my first win was enough to allow me a third place medal and not deny myself the souvenir. Also, the two matches allowed me to sweat off enough to ensure I could eat and still make weight the next day. As I left the podium, medal in hand, I went over to see my bracket for the next day. My first match was with the Swiss guy who just beat me.

My Purple Belt Statement Tour was starting off mediocre at best and now I had to refight the man who just killed me, the Swiss guy.

I decided to avoid pulling guard and instead I would fight for top. That was the plan for the rematch. It was the right decision. He shot for the leg, I sprawled and stuffed him. I passed into mount and finished him with a gi choke. It was a surprising and great start to my second day.

Combat sports are interesting in that two guys can logistically be the same size but not the same size once they're on the mat head-to-head…which brings me to my next match against the Polish guy. He was my height and weight, but not the same size at all, not by a long shot. I would guess my body fat to be in the twenty percent range, and his seemed to be in the nonexistent range. When I grabbed him, all I could feel was rock under his sleeve. There was nothing to grab onto, nothing to sink your fingers into for more grip. He shot into a position known as half guard. This was a first for me in competition.

When he did that it gave me an advantage point, which is why it is unusual, but not unheard of. He had a plan and was executing it to perfection. I held on, but within a minute I was on my back and he had side control. I kept him off the submission, but lost on points. I took another third place medal home from the trip, but I wasn't feeling overly impressive in my showing.

That night I went with some fellow competitors to a big steak dinner and then hit the clubs of Lisbon. I barely made it back to the hotel. Thank God for taxis. The next day I went for lunch with all of the Megaton affiliates and then went sightseeing by myself. The following morning I was headed for London for some more sightseeing. In looking over my hotel bill before dashing off to London, I noticed a 4:00 A.M. phone call charge to a Phoenix number that I didn't immediately recognize. Drunk Mike had drunk-dialed the beautiful Tiramisu Girl, or more accurately, Drunk Mike had drunk-dialed her from Europe!! (My alter ego goes by the name Drunk Mike or Mayhem Mike depending on the deeds that he left for Sober Mike to clean up.) How in the fuck did Drunk Mike figure that shit out? He had to have her number memorized? Or take it off his cell and then dial on the hotel phone? Drunk Mike is ambitious. He is a crafty bastard. I wonder how much damage he did with that phone call. It'd be nice if Drunk Mike would have taken a more active role in preparing Sober Mike for jiu-jitsu and would have spent less time screwing around. Leaving with more gold and less bronze and arriving back home with the purple belt in my pocket would have been sweet! That inner monologue haunted me all the way to London.

Chapter 23

*"I always see about six scuffles a night when I come to
San Francisco. That's one of the town's charms."*
—Erroll Flynn

Streets of San Francisco

On April 13, 2011, Paris Augusta stepped onto a bus in San Francisco and sat down without paying for the ride. Not long into his journey two police men, an officer and a reserve officer came and escorted Paris Augusta off of the bus and proceeded to write him a citation. Augusta defied them, turned and walked away. The officer and his reserve officer commanded the twenty-three year old to stop, but Augusta did not comply.[22]

For years my own father was a reserve officer. Generally, reserve officers are part-time sworn officers who have certification, and while trained are not as trained as actual officers. Reserve officer is technically a community service position. These people generally do this work in their off hours from a real job, or are retirees helping with traffic control, or are folks considering being an officer and want the experience before committing to the police academy. Typically, a reserve officer is used to assist the full-time police officer, but they neither patrol nor respond to calls on their own. Reserve officers are not generally equipped for battle.

So, it's of little surprise that when the two officers caught up to Augusta and he turned and punched the lead officer, then tackled and continued to pummel him, that the reserve officer had trouble controlling the cheap-shot attack of this aggressive, defiant twenty-three year old. I am sure, given enough time, the two officers would have eventually subdued the assailant, but we will never really know. What Augusta didn't realize was that he had made his attack on the officers in front of a jiu-jitsu academy that was just letting out a class.

Jiu-jitsu instructor Pedro Arrigoni saw the scuffle outside the gym and reacted. According to Pedro, he didn't see a cop being beaten up, he saw a person in danger. Jiu-jitsu is respect, respect for humans. Pedro took the back of the suspect and sunk in a rear naked choke. Pedro's belief is that jiu-jitsu is more than just a choke, it's control and applying just what is needed.

Pedro had Augusta held securely in position when he asked, "Are you going to be cool?"

Augusta readily agreed. The cops were then able to jump up and handcuff him. [23]

Jumbled video footage of the incident had clear audio where, sadly, several bystanders screamed at Pedro saying, "You ain't no fucking police!" and, "Mother fucker! You going to get your ass whooped!" and, "Why you got him in a choke hold, man!? That's illegal, mother fucker!" and, "I know where you live, you come on my block, I got two niggas…"[24]

In his interview, Pedro recalled being called "white boy" by the bystanders. What you didn't see from Pedro was an exaggerated angry response toward the assailant or the taunting bystanders because there was none. He is a calm and composed Brazilian who happened to also be a purple belt Brazilian Jiu-jitsu artist.

This story is another great example of jiu-jitsu allowing the practitioner to apply just enough force for the situation. With a pure striker, all he has is the punch and the punch is an all-in type of engagement. If you throw a partial punch or a light punch, you don't subdue an attacker, you just piss them off. The other choice is to strike for the knock out, which can result in extreme injury and death, or worse yet, hurting yourself and further enabling the attack. As Pedro stated, jiu-jitsu is about respect and control.

This story made me think that it might be a good plan if every police officer knew jiu-jitsu. Just a thought.

Chapter 24

"From this day to the ending of the world,
But we in it shall be remembered-
We few, we happy few, we band of brothers;
For he today that sheds his blood with me
Shall be my brother;"
—St. Crispin's Day Speech, *Henry V* (1599)
William Shakespeare

Back to the Beach

SPRING 2008 MEANT IT WAS BACK TO THE PAN AMS. MARKSPRAY AND I made our preparations. We were to head out, get a nice place rented on Hermosa Beach, fight, hang out on the beach, have some cocktails and meet some chicks. Protocol. With this in mind, a hotel room in Manhattan Beach was booked. It was a perfect storm. In addition to my usual jiu-jitsu travel companions, my brother, Glenn-Crazyland's newest resident-decided to meet us there. Greg had decided to enter the tournament, too. And to top off the list, my Uncle John had entered as well. When Markspray showed up for the drive across the desert, he had his son and this white belt named Jay. All I really knew of Jay was that he had given me a black eye the week before.

Markspray's son joined us because he had gotten suspended from middle school that morning. The boy had been having trouble with a group of kids who had been taunting him all year. This kid was truly sweet, which is probably why he got bullied. Markspray had suspected a fight would erupt sooner or later, and so he had worked with his son with some pads and taught him striking techniques in addition to the kid's regular jiu-jitsu training. That morning the fight had broken out in the cafeteria. Markspray's son threw a combination his dad had taught him, getting the bully in a headlock while continuing to throw strikes to the face. Both kids got suspended. Apparently, a teacher and security guard had pulled Markspray aside to express that it was standard procedure that they had had to suspend both kids, but that they were thrilled his son had taken it to the bully. But Markspray felt it was only fair to punish his son for getting suspended. So, he had to go to the beach with us; that was the punishment. I believe a valuable lesson was learned that day. And can't help but wish that Markspray had been my dad. You will not fight your brother to near-death in the kitchen, till your shaky and sweaty and out of breath and bloody and begging for mercy. You will hop in a car with several fun-loving, thrill-seeking, competitive guys with a zest for life and you will hang out on the beach and at a jiu-jitsu tournament. Take that, son!

Markspray is an "angle guy." So before we left we had to fill the back of my Hummer with cases of wine to drop off at some restaurant. This was in exchange for a hotel room in Manhattan Beach. Hell, between the weight of the wine and the poor gas mileage the Hummer got, we definitely lost money on that deal. I think this was my first foray into smuggling, which brings me to the other passenger in the car, Jay.

Jay was a strong, good looking guy in his late twenties. He had an interesting array of tats and a shaved head which made him look hard. And he was a quiet guy, as guys with big muscles, shaved heads and tats often are. When I had rolled with him, he brought a lot of dynamic power to the grapple and was not going to quit unless he was absolutely dead to rights. As Markspray and I made our familiar trip through the desert, we bantered away which was par for the course. After about two hours, Jay chimed in, "I usually keep to myself, but you guys are really nice and cool."

We smiled and nodded back at Jay. We enjoyed being called cool.

Then Jay added casually, "I just got out of prison, seven years for smuggling marijuana."

I looked at my Rolex. Fuck, now I gotta keep an eye on my shit. Mark and I flashed each other a glance, he was thinking the same thing.

We reached Manhattan Beach. The Hummer and the designated covered parking were a tight fit, but I thought nothing of it as a Hummer generally seems bigger than it actually is. Hmm. Anyway, Markspray called for the wine pickup as we checked in. In the fashion of unloading a stash of Moonshine, Markspray's son, Jay (the convicted felon) and I unloaded the cases of wine into "the pickup car." Then we slapped the back of that getaway vehicle for good measure and it sped off. I closed the back of the Hummer and was dumbstruck to see that the removal of the load made the automobile significantly taller. We could not pull out of the parking space. The Hummer was above the height limit. I am not an idiot. Not all of the time. Just ask me. But

I've never thought to actually read height restrictions as it was a fucking Hummer, not a semi-truck carrying fucking palm trees to a freshly erected retirement community in Phoenix. Because I am not a complete idiot, I had everyone take a tire. We immediately began letting the air out of them to lower the height of the Hummer. There it is-my engineering degree in action, yet again.

We were one day from the tournament.

My weight was a little high so I found a Bikram yoga studio within walking distance. The three of them were looking at me like I was a faggy hippie. So I explained that the room is one hundred degrees. You do all these extreme yoga positions and I've lost about seven pounds of water weight every time I've done it.

They weren't sold.

So I added, "Oh! And there's a ton of hot, sweaty chicks wearing tight clothing and twisting into all those crazy poses in a room that's wall-to-wall mirrors."

With that, we all headed to the yoga studio, including Markspray's son. He had to go where we went. He was grounded, after all. Poor bastard.

Yoga is supposed to be meditative and calming. I think stoic is the word. The mirrors, which at first sounded completely awesome and God sent, became a focal point evoking uncontrollable laughter from our group. We tried not to make eye contact, but the mirrors made it impossible. Markspray in a half moon sent me into a fit of giggles— junior high girl giggles. Then Jay, the felon started giggling, and of course the pre-teen started out-and-out laughing. Our attractive female instructor attempted to regroup the class. But, by the time we got to standing eagle, there was no hope. Mark's son couldn't keep his balance and was falling all over the back of the room, which seemed like he was falling all over the room thanks to all of the mirrors. And, before we knew it, our attractive female instructor became infected with an acute case of the giggles, too. The people who were there for a serious, introspective, meditative workout were screwed. For those of us who came to lose weight and have a good time, the pounds were off! My face hurt from laughing, or from trying not to laugh. And we had collected several phone numbers for the weekend, including the instructor's. It's moments like that that create bonds, for I was no longer concerned about Jay's criminal past. We had just spent ninety minutes sweating, stretching and mostly giggling our asses off through a Bikram Yoga class, just my buddy, his kid and the felon. We were good now.

The next morning, we all took a short jog along the beach and stopped by a coffee shop. Markspray's son could eat whatever he wanted. And so he did. He ate this gigantic breakfast, a breakfast fit for two linebackers, right in front of me while I mulled over a piece of toast and half of an egg. In fact, Markspray's son hit his food so hard, fast and messily, it was like he had just picked up a cheeseburger after a night of heavy drinking.

"Goddamn, Markspray. Your kid is Hasslehoffing the shit out of those pancakes!" I was pissed and starving, plus he looked happy which pissed me off even more.

My tone was apparently irrelevant because that was all it took. The giggles were back in full force, which was nice, they squashed most of my anger and the butterflies. Shortly thereafter, it was tournament time.

As we walked through the parking lot of the Pan Ams, I spotted my uncle's truck. We walked up because it was running. There he sat, with sweats and a hoodie on. The man was over sixty years old and cutting weight for his fight. Shit. I hope I'm that cool at sixty. His match was one of the first. He had to be the oldest fighter in the tournament. His opponent was at least ten years younger. They battled relentlessly for top. The weight cut began to have an effect on my uncle's calves, they were cramping. He started hobbling around like Ralph Macchio in The Karate Kid. The age disparity coupled with his willingness to fight on-in spite of his condition-had drawn a large crowd. And everyone was cheering for him, again, like The Karate Kid. But this wasn't a movie and he ultimately lost. He lost the fight, but had won the complete admiration of a Brazilian jiu-jitsu crowd, which is no small feat. I was proud to be his nephew.

Greg showed up for my match, he had lost the day before, so he was out, but he was still in great spirits. Once again, I believed that this tournament was mine to lose. The first match started. We high-fived and engaged. I had taken a rules seminar and had begun the process of tilting the referee toward my favor. In jiu-jitsu, you must stay within the boundaries of the mat. Too many times being shoved off of the mat results in penalties. At lower belts, the IBJJF leniently enforces this rule, meaning they don't typically penalize the competitor. However, I believed that at the very least, in the event of a tie, that could factor in the referee's decision. After the third time of moving my opponent off of the mat, he got smart and pulled guard.

With three minutes, my opponent worked my arm across my body (A move that I prefer when I am in guard). Because I knew this, I was able to stuff it, but not do much more. This battle went on for three minutes. To the average spectator it appeared to be a very boring match. But to us, this battle for an inch was everything. It was a simple sweep or a pass that was to determine the winner. The match ended zero-to-zero with no advantage. And I didn't sell it enough to the referee. I lost. And that was that.

Some may question my resolve to win, and it was disappointing, but acceptance is part of the bigger jiu-jitsu picture. It was now time to have some fun. Markspray, his son my brother, Glenn, Greg and I headed down to Hermosa Beach for dinner and drinks. Jay made other plans. The fun of the night made up for any ill feelings toward all of the losses. And, Markspray had done incredibly well, taking first in his bracket. After sushi, Markspray and Glenn called it a night, but Greg and I were just getting started. By the end of the night, we had met some girls who invited us to the beach the following day. They were professional beach volleyball players and were spending a sunny warm Sunday practicing. From a couple of athletes to a couple of cute others, it seemed silly not to go and root them on. I can't tell you how the Pan Ams went that Sunday, but Greg and I went home the following morning with a tan and a smile.

Chapter 25

*"I like to wake up knowing that I could
kick my own ass yesterday."*
—Unknown

Canadian with Disability Acts

IN NOVEMBER OF 2010, A YOUNG MAN ENTERED THE FOOD STOP IN
Vancouver, Canada and tried to pass a counterfeit fifty dollar bill. The
clerk, Cindy Grewal, recognized the bill as a fake, informed the man
that it was counterfeit, said that she was calling the police, but also told
him that he was free to just leave. Rather than seizing the opportunity to run, he walked behind the counter and tried to take the bill back.

In a close-by aisle, Larry Skopnik was tuned into this dialogue. A
decade earlier, Larry had had an ATV accident that left him without
the use of his legs. Larry was in a wheelchair. Just as Cindy had shoved
the young man backwards, Larry wheeled his way up to the register.
He managed to grab the attacker from behind and pull him into a rear
naked choke on his lap in the wheelchair. Because Larry couldn't lock
him in place with his legs, the assailant spun around. So Larry effi-
ciently readjusted his hold into a guillotine choke causing the young
man to rear backwards. They both hit the floor. By this time, other

patrons had come to his aid and they helped detain the man.[25] But Larry had heart and guts. And you can't teach that. Larry's the reason the guy was caught.

The articles and news footage gave no indications that Larry ever trained jiu-jitsu or MMA, but his movements and adjustments were spot on. And given his condition, it's a story worth telling.

Chapter 26

"It never always gets worse."
—An "Ultra-Runner" Saying

Crap! It's worse!

I READ AN ARTICLE ON A SOUTHWEST FIGHT MAGAZINE ABOUT ULTRA running and later read about it again in Sam Sheridan's book, *A Fighter's Mind*. These runners have events where they run a marathon distance a day for a week and events where they run 50 miles or 100 miles in one day. The point is that while in such extreme events, the mind will start to believe that because it's hard right now, it's only going to get worse, but if you can keep going, it doesn't always get worse.

Our Band of Brothers returned from the Pan Ams a happy few, Markspray with his gold medal, my uncle with the admiration of the fans, and Greg and me with our volleyball girls. During the drive back, Jay mentioned he lived near my ex-sister-in-law's house and that he had even met my father-in-law. It is a small world. A few days after returning, I asked Kristin, my sister-in-law if she knew Jay. She said, "You mean my neighbor Jay who the cops sent a team after last night, including a helicopter? Yeah, I know Jay. He was arrested."

Over the next few months and into the summer I could feel the economy tightening. My company was still profitable, but our big projects were ending and new projects were smaller and shorter in duration and getting paid required relentless calls to clients unwilling or unable to pay. Markspray, Eric and I would meet for jiu-jitsu at lunch and spend any surplus time talking about how hard development was becoming, consoling each other and speculating on when the worst of the recession would hit. Early into that summer of '08, we had speculated that there would be six months worth of a recession period. Man, were we off. However, so was the Federal Reserve as well as thousands of Ivy League bankers with PhDs; so I won't kick myself too hard. My payroll was one hundred thousand per month and the cash was getting harder and harder to generate and collect. The economic faucet had been on full blast for so many years I couldn't conceive of it shutting off completely, which is exactly what it did.

I believe in God. I am not religious. I don't go to church and I don't feel compelled to go to church. But, I do have this thing I do when life pushes down on me hard. I help someone. Maybe it's a karma-like belief, but I just think that if you can show generosity when the world is giving you none, it somehow changes things. Fine, fuck you. You're right. I'm a superstitious bastard.

Anyway, about this time I got a call from Jay who was out on bail. He asked me to meet him at Megaton's, and then he asked me for a job. Given my struggles, my first reaction was no. He needed the job as a condition of his bail. After class, while driving home, I called him and said I could give him a part-time job at minimum wage. It was honestly the best I could offer. This was me saying Fuck You to the universe. Jay was looking straight at another ten years in prison. The law had caught up to him for running marijuana between Mexico and Chicago. I thought, shit, if I was in his shoes, I would hope someone would help me. I even wrote a letter to the judge asking for leniency. He didn't get it, though, but he took my lame job offer.

On the first day, his task was to ride with me while I went from meeting to meeting and just take notes. We were having tacos at lunch when he confessed that he knew his sentence would be long once his trial was over. And then he said that at one point he had had over one and a half million dollars buried in the desert. But, when the feds intercepted and confiscated his truck with the load of marijuana, he had to dig up the money to pay off the Mexicans so they wouldn't kill him.

I could relate to a man risking it all, having the millions and in a flash losing them. Just a year earlier, Sarah and I were in talks to sell the company for several million. My words to Sarah after one of the meetings was, "I would rather go broke than work for those assholes." That which I had manifested was before me.

So Jay and I ate tacos, each of us with our problems, I believed his to be slightly worse than mine and I think if you're going to be worth a million and then lose it, then my way was better. At least my way didn't involve a decade of jail time.

I finally said, "Wouldn't it have been nice to just have a job as a greeter at Wal-Mart, and train jiu-jitsu and do nothing else?"

He smiled and agreed. I went to the Worlds by myself that summer; lost my match, and picked up what I called the Thousand Dollar

T-shirt—approximate price of hotel, gas, food and registration.

The banks soon began to tighten revolving lines of credit. This began to kill my float and the layoffs began. I was laying off old friends who had worked for me for years. I told the staff that they could come back to the office to prepare resumes and I would write letters of recommendation. It was depressing.

I had three tiers of cuts: the easy cuts, the hard cuts and then the are-you-fucking-kidding-me cuts. The easy cuts were temporary staff and people who were hired for a project that was ending. They knew it was temporary. The hard cuts were good people, but people who were no longer profitable. In that final tier was Greg, my great buddy, Greg. I nearly burned to death with Greg while wandering around the grounds of a volcano in Hawaii. Greg: the guy who on the very same trip nearly drowned scuba diving in four feet of water (just stand up Greg). Greg: the man who taught me how to meet women. Greg: a friend who would do me one more favor even as he graciously accepted the axe.

Greg was at the office about a week after I let him go. He was preparing his resumé when he told me about an offer from an insurance company to inspect hurricane damage in Houston for $70/hour for as many hours as he could work. He thought I ought to investigate it, too, what with my company downsizing so drastically and all. I just let the guy go and he still had my back.

I billed out at $140/hour at the time, but only about ten-to-twenty hours per week. I went home and the numbers kept running through my head. If I went out and busted out twelve-to-fourteen hour days for a few months, my family and business could make it through this recession. I went online to see if I could find similar opportunities, and I did.

For me, the job was working as a contract engineer for FEMA, helping communities get back on their feet who were hit by hurricanes Ike and Gustav. Aaron and I were in the last group accepted. FEMA deployed me for training in Virginia for ten days and then to Lafayette, Louisiana. Aaron ended up in Ohio and then Houston.

The speed of the deployment from the initial interview to my flight into Virginia to start the job was just over a week. I secured the office; Sarah would run it and watch our kids. My father-in-law and mother-in-law were both very supportive; they were on standby to help. I went to train one last time and my knee popped. My cartilage had torn in my left knee this time. I could walk and there was no time for surgery or even an MRI. This was the Universe saying "fuck you" back.

I had needed to speak with Megaton as well. For at least six months I was going to be MIA. There were loose ends that needed tying up. I was missing the promotions, for one, so I just went ahead and asked him for the purple belt.

"No, Seempson. How long have you been a blue belt?" he inquired, as if I had just gotten it.

"Two and a half years. And I don't think I'm going to be around for the Christmas party." I replied, deflated.

"You need to wait. It is not the time." He was right. I did not need to go trotting into some unknown school with my newly minted purple belt and a bad knee. A newbie purple belt in an unknown school would get tested. It sounded so sweet, though. The idea of going on this new, unknown adventure with a purple belt in hand felt somehow uplifting. I'm embarking on a new phase in life-one that hadn't entered my mind as a married man. The idea of leaving my family for months for work, in order to stay comfortably afloat never occurred to me during the "I dos," and having a new badge of honor, a purple badge of honor seemed fitting. It really did.

Shit. Crap. He was right.

Chapter 27

"If a fighter doesn't know jiu-jitsu,
He will lose for sure,
But even if he knows jiu-jitsu,
It is not a guarantee that he will win."
—Hai Tran
Brown Belt NOLA BJJ

Bus Stop Beating

ON JUNE 8, 2012, A YOUNG TEENAGE COUPLE WAS SITTING AT A BUS BENCH in Calgary, Canada when a pack of five other teenagers randomly attacked. They brutally beat and robbed them. The incident took place on the 9600 block of MacLeod Trail, a nice part of town that has a strip mall along with other shops and restaurants.

Nick Ring, a thirty-three year old MMA fighter had just stopped for a coffee at the nearby Starbucks after his yoga class (I am not the only martial artist in yoga studios) and witnessed the tail-end of the robbery. He and an unknown Good Samaritan ran to check on the victims and then went in pursuit of the attackers, eventually pinning one of the male teenagers down. The Good Samaritan held that assailant on the ground while Nick called the police. The other young felons initially pleaded with Nick to let their friend go and then even challenged him to a one-on-one fight. They didn't even show that kind of honor to their victims.

I'd have paid fifty bucks to watch that fight.

In interviews following the incident, Nick acknowledged that the Good Samaritan had done most of the work, but added, "I saw these little punk cowards picking on defenseless people and I knew they needed to come to justice. They looked like they came right from a rap video. They watch too many movies and they obviously think they're a lot tougher than they are. They think it's okay to rob people, apparently, but it's not. This was a situation where they were just punks, and not very tough people. No one with an ounce of bravery would consider any such actions."[26]

The police eventually arrested all five suspects in the attack, thanks to Nick King and the Good Samaritan.

Chapter 28

"If you're going through hell, keep going."
—Winston Churchill

Race to Lafayette

WHILE IN FEMA TRAINING IN VIRGINIA, I HAD MADE FRIENDS WITH A bunch of guys who all seemed to be excited to be on the road. There was a sense of adventure among all of us-going somewhere felt so much better than riding out the recession at home. It gave the sense of being proactive about the issue, or maybe it felt like we could outrun it. But, by the time we all got deployed, that camaraderie had basically evaporated, as it was just me and one other guy who ended up together in Baton Rouge. His name was Stu. He was about ten years older than me, but we were both originally from California, so there was a familiarity.

We sat in a semi-vacated, gutted building that was formerly a department store. Literally, for ten days, we sat at a metal table waiting for orders. Every day we would arrive there for 8:00 A.M., sit, leave at 12:00 P.M. for lunch. Then we'd return at 12:30 P.M., sit and then leave at 4:30 P.M. On the eighth day, four FEMA managers from various parts of Louisiana came and introduced themselves. They said we'd be assigned to one of them. All of them were nice enough, but you can always tell which one you really know you would get along with the best. His name was Dan. So, Stu and I sat quietly, saying a little prayer that we would be able to stick together and go with Dan. By day ten our prayers were answered. Dan called both of our names. He pulled us aside and said about eight more of us would work out of hotel rooms in Lafayette and the rest would work out of the little office in Lake Charles. But the first few guys to have their equipment and show up at the Lake Charles office would be sent to Lafayette. Without words, Stu and I were already in synch. This was the FEMA version of the Amazing Race.

Getting anything from the government, even while working for them is a feat. We went at it, and within forty-eight hours we had our gear and were hauling ass toward Lake Charles. We ended up being the second and third to arrive and were sent to Lafayette to work out of our hotel rooms. Yes! Although I had never done this type of work, Dan made me a manager in charge of the recovery of three Parishes (Parishes are the same as Counties).

On November 1, 2008, I arrived in Lafayette, Louisiana. I walked into the Marriot Residence Inn, threw my bag on the floor, fell onto the bed and for the first time in months felt like I would be able to row my boat to safety. From start of the recession to this moment it had been only three months, but a lot had happened in three short months. Jay had been sentenced to ten years in prison. And as for my training partners? Markspray's Wyoming land ranches were not selling and he was dabbling with foreclosure. Eric's large development company was down to two retail sites and he was headed to Colorado. Aaron was in Ohio working for FEMA as well, and every single one of our homes were upside down.

When I had left, Markspray gave me a bit of a pep-talk and made two key points. He said, "Mike, this is what dads do, they go out and they earn and do whatever it takes. Your kids may not understand it or like it, but that's our task." He followed it up by telling me not to hoard my per diem like it was pay, but to accept that I was on the road, away from home and use it to treat myself well, to have a nice meal here and there and see the place. It was solid advice.

But beyond all that, the first order of business was to find a Brazilian jiu-jitsu school. I found a place called Cajun Karate run by a BJJ black belt named Micah Lopez. I sent Micah an email and he responded very positively.

There's this thing humans do, well, men do, women probably do it, too, and I don't think it's just at jiu-jitsu schools. We're wired to be suspicious of new people. If a guy walks into a BJJ school and has never trained, if he comes in street clothes or a perfectly pressed gi with a white belt, there is practically no scrutiny from the majority of the class. It's like being a pre-schooler. You're just a baby. What harm can he do? *Actually, you're kind of cute all uncoordinated and chubby.* That's what the majority of the class thinks. But, if you walk in with a blue belt and some stripes on that belt, and that belt and the gi have battle scars, you will be tested. There are all of these ego dances going on at the same time.

First of all, the school wants to be known as a quality school, so there is the school's reputation. Secondly, there is the guy you're going to roll against; he wants to be good, too. And you're new to him so he's unsure of how to handle you, so he throws down more aggressively than usual. Thirdly, there's your own reputation. You want people to know that you represent the belt you have around your waist. And, lastly, there is the reputation of the school which is displayed on the patch on your back. You want the new place to know that your original school also produces quality BJJ practitioners. And, also, and this may be just me (but I think it's most jiu-jitsu guys), I want to balance or manage those four egos by displaying a certain amount of respect for the place that has allowed me into their home. Be a proper guest, I remind myself of that every time.

The first night at Cajun Karate, Micah was finishing up with a kids' karate class. I waltzed into the other studio where kick boxing was wrapping up. Some BJJ guys were hanging around the perimeter, waiting on class. I was able to check them out and vice versa. This is the first time I felt total relief about not having the purple belt, especially given my knee. Although anyone who trains knew that my gi was a giveaway as to my time on the mat. My lapels and belt were frayed from all the hours and the stripes on my belt were maxed out at four and were peeling off from all of the rolling.

Class started with some stretching during which Micah very graciously said, "This is Mike, he is from Phoenix and trains at Megaton. He is here working for several months. While he is here, he has a home with us."

I was unsure what my knee could handle, but the test was about to begin.

I remember three extremely large white belts, a father and two sons. I believe both the boys played football for the Ragin Cajuns at the University of Louisiana. The father put in a fast request to roll with me. They were all white belts, but they were pushing 250 easily, which meant that I couldn't give them much quarter. I tapped the father with a quick arm bar and then went to more traditional bread and butter stuff. I finished out the round on cruise control, trying to keep it respectful. The father then immediately requested that I roll with one of the sons. The boy was so strong, but I focused on my technique. I was battle hardened from all the tournaments. Four rounds and a thousand pounds of meat later, my first day at Micah's was done. This was going to be a great place to train.

One month after arriving, I was at a bar with Stu. It was a Friday night; it was also the Megaton Christmas party back home. Markspray called from the event and put Megaton on the phone, "Congratulations, Seempson! You are a purple belt!"

That was not how I planned for that to go down. But at this point in my life, nothing really was. And I was elated. I told my new buddy Stu, even though I knew he had no idea what this moment meant. And I didn't have the words to explain it out, the journey, the licks, my bad knees, Crazyland, the peaks and troughs...only those who train can know. I just had a smile plastered to my face originating from pure happiness, the feeling that comes with high achievement. I couldn't wait to tell Micah, I knew he would "get it."

Blue Belt Accomplishments:

Four Years ✓✓✓✓

Ass Kicked ✓

Humbled ✓

Nonsmoker ✓

9 Tournaments ✓✓✓✓✓✓✓✓✓

9 Wins ✓✓✓✓✓✓✓✓✓

8 Losses 👎 👎 👎 👎 👎 👎 👎 👎

1 Gold Medal ✓

2 Silver Medals ✓✓

4 Bronze Medals ✓✓✓✓

Black Eyes ✓

Knee Surgery (right) 👎

Self-esteem ✓

Nearly 3,000 hours of jiu-jitsu ✓

Six Pack Abs for my Girlfriend 👎

Girlfriend 👎✓👎

Drive through the desert in the summer with the heat on to
    lose the last two pounds ✓

215 Pounds ✓

Chapter 29

"I like a man who grins when he fights."
—Winston Churchill

Geaux

As I settled into my routine in Lafayette, I noticed my temporary life there was beginning to remind me of Crazyland. I was drinking too much, chasing too many chicks, generally out of control. I knew the cause was being away from my kids, the deep economic struggles and breaking up with a girlfriend for whom I cared for very deeply. I missed Megaton Academy, the source of my stability, my church, my therapist, my gym, my club. As generous and friendly and accepting as the new surroundings and school were, it was not home. There was no Megaton, Luka, Markspray, Greg, Eric or Aaron. And my employees who I had seen every day for years were gone, as well. They were my work family. Mostly, though, I missed my kids terribly. I've never been away from them for months. The divorce was a big enough transition. To go from a full-time to a part-time parent just sucked. Now it seemed as if they'd vanished from my life. About an hour a week on the phone with the two of them wasn't doing much to fill the pit that had gouged itself into my heart.

I wasn't a tourist of Crazyland anymore. On my first tour I had purchased the full adventure package, I had learned to speak the language fluently and had adapted to the culture like I was a goddamned native. It would not hold me hostage like that a second time. I was too aware of it this time around. I refocused and set goals: maintain my conditioning, maintain the weight loss or even lose a few more pounds, limit my drinking, learn something new, keep training, get the knee fixed, and be the best FEMA contractor on Gustav/Ike so I could get to New Orleans. Getting to New Orleans meant working the Hurricane Katrina catastrophe, which fascinated me, but more importantly, it meant being able to fly home on weekends.

The really bitchin' part of training in Lafayette, though, was meeting all of these guys who wanted to be professional MMA fighters. If Las Vegas was the place where a majority of fighters go to refine their art, Lafayette, and other small towns in Louisiana was like finding the source waters of the Colorado River—the place was where they all got their start.

One night, a pretty bartender in Lafayette saw my jiu-jitsu shirt and asked if I was a fighter. I told her I was visiting from Phoenix and her response was, "Why would you visit here? The only thing to do around here is drink, fuck and fight." This culture, the drink, fuck and fight culture that defined my new home-base was something I could grow accustomed to quite easily, which was just another reason for me to focus on the fighting part of it.

I kept this promise to myself, at least partially. I started kick boxing, and my weight dropped to two hundred and ten pounds. I began outpacing everyone at FEMA. However, the knee surgery would have to wait until the summer, and boredom drinking became a constant obstacle for me to overcome. At the time, there was only a hand full of purple belts or higher in the Lafayette area, so I would come in and roll with the fighters to help them get ready for their fights, and then cruise to the nearest local pub and drink till midnight. This got my knee extra ripe for surgery, but it was just too cool of an opportunity to pass up. Plus, it curbed the boredom drinking substantially.

Due to my increase in training and working, there was not a lot of time for much more. Even still, I began to work on something that I called HOTH. I never considered myself very good at meeting women. And, since I was between girlfriends and was alone in a new place, I began to not just interact with more women, but I started to study different concepts of meeting women and then practiced putting them into action. This wasn't necessarily about getting laid; it was more about trying to understand the art of meeting women, and to also address my biggest fear, which was the initial approach. It was jiu-jitsu of a different kind.

HOTH is based on something Markspray told me once when I was headed to the Hyatt Regency in Scottsdale for a little staycation (yes, I sorta lived there for a few weeks while I was in Crazyland). Markspray had said, "You know Mike, the Hyatt has the hottest help in town. You gotta go poolside and go hit on the help. You won't regret it." Thus the term HOTH was born: Hit On The Help.

This may sound sleazy, but it's not, it's genius. And it's the best way to get your feet wet when it comes to approaching women. The "help" are often stuck with you long after you flirt, so it's critical to make it count. After years of being single and hanging out with single friends, I began to see that some guys were just naturally talented at this, and others simply were not. And very little of it actually had to do with the way you look, much like in jiu-jitsu. And like jiu-jitsu, some guys were trained and elegant in their approach, while others were clumsy and brutal, and others were altogether afraid of the arena, so they generally avoided it at all costs. I've always put myself into that last category. I played it off like I was letting the ladies come to me, but truthfully I was a pussy when it came to the approach.

I began reading books on everything related to the pick up from Revelations (of course by the guys from *The Pickup Artist* on VH1) to books on body language. I would actually turn on a reality show, hit the mute button, watch the body language and try and determine the dynamics without sound, I would then rewind it to see how closely I was able to read the body language.

Since I was short on time and couldn't use what little time I did have for late night clubbing, I was discovering ways to effectively latch onto real, live opportunities in any environment, when they happened, wherever they happened. This wasn't me wanting to learn techniques for picking up drunk girls and this wasn't to pump my ego so I could say to my friends, "hey, guys, check out my new trick," and then discretely point to exhibit A (the hot brunette on my arm). This was about learning and perfecting a new art.

The system was working. I was getting lots of numbers, meeting all sorts of new ladies and going on dates. After all of the reading/training, I was no black belt, but I felt like a solid blue. But just because I knew a few pick up techniques didn't mean I would always pick up the girl, just like in jiu-jitsu. Just because I knew the sport, didn't mean I could always get my opponent to tap. But, like the time when I rolled against the wrestler, I was starting to recognize patterns and to seize moments.

I think one of the more fun moments of this new art in motion came for me on a trip back to Phoenix. My ex had taken the kids on vacation, so for the first few days home I was alone. I asked a friend to pick me up from the airport, she said she would, but ended up being a no show. As usual, I was exhausted from the flight, so I called her feeling a little irritated. "Kelly, it's Mike, I am at the airport. Are you coming?"

Flatly, Kelly replied, "Mike, I went to meet my friend Beth in Scottsdale for happy hour and at this point I shouldn't drive."

"Cool. I'll get a cab."

"If you want to join us, we are at Zuzu in the Valley Ho," she added.

That was nice of her.

I was tired, but as I got into the cab, I told him to take me to the Valley Ho. No pun intended; that's really the name of the place.

The Valley Ho is a retro hotel located in Scottsdale that was originally built in 1956 and looks like it came straight out of an Austin Powers movie. Zuzu's is known in the Phoenix Valley for its martinis and Scottsdale babes.

Kelly was the ex-wife of a quasi-friend from years prior. I was no longer friends with him, but Kelly and I had crossed paths, spoke of our divorces and had been meeting for drinks and conversations off and on for the past several years. We weren't like that (what you're thinking). I was not interested in her. Don't get me wrong, she was attractive, but she was blond. I'm a brunette man by nature. And I honestly can say there really was no vibe for her, either.

I arrived at the Valley Ho with my travel backpack and nothing else. As I entered the lobby, a pretty brunette walked by and I asked her the time.

"Ten thirty," she replied with a smile.

Inside Zuzu I found the girls at a table. I set my backpack down. As I opened it up to find my wallet, Kelly saw the books I was hauling, she was particularly drawn to the one on picking up women. I think it was called, How to Pick Up Women. Anyway, she grabbed that one without an invitation. She read the title out loud to Beth and they both started laughing and berating me (never mind that the other book was The Catcher in the Rye—which I pointed out). They didn't care. The ribbing began.

"You really aren't reading this crap, are you Mike?! This doesn't work; why would you need this?!"

I maintained composure, even though I was slightly embarrassed by being caught with the book in my possession. I began to explain that the "crap" in those books does in fact work and that more guys should read them. Kelly and her friend were both being hot chicks. They've never had had to approach anyone cold, and even if they had, they were hot chicks, how hard could it have been?

"Calm down and listen before you judge, there is good information that doesn't guarantee a kill, but tilts the table considerably, like counting cards in blackjack."

They kept right on giggling.

"Okay girls, look around this bar, if your goal was to get laid, which girl would you hit on and why?"

Kelly jumped in without thought, "That's easy, the girl in the skinny jeans and navy blue top."

"Yes! She's got big fake boobs and she likes to show them off." Beth chimed in.

"Interesting. That would not have been my choice. I would have gone with her friend. She is wearing bright colors and her complexion is clear. The girl in blue looks like she's using make-up to cover a couple of blemishes. While bright colors and a clear complexion indicate that the friend may be ovulating, which means she would be hornier."

Almost instinctively, Kelly and Beth disagreed with me. But their body language indicated that they were suddenly feeling self-conscious of their own brightly colored clothing. I could tell they wanted to hear more as indicated by another change in their body language. Their arms had become uncrossed and they were both turned into me and leaning in. I did not mention this to them, I merely took note of it.

Then Beth challenged me, "Go hit on her."

"If you don't mind, I am going to hit on the brunette right there instead. She is more my type. And she's alone and also brightly dressed. If I get her digits, will that be enough to get you two off my ass?" I quipped.

They nodded in agreement.

I went in.

The brunette was at the bar, right next to our table. She was the girl from the lobby from whom I had requested the time. I was putting into play all sorts of techniques. This one was the "re-meet," where you meet a girl through a simple and safe conversation (request for time) and then re-meet her. In her mind, she feels like she knows you.

I approached the slot at the bar next to her, but faced away from her and still chatted it up with Kelly. Then I accidentally bumped into her ever so slightly and turned to apologize while feigning initial recognition. "Oh excuse me. Oh, hey, it's Time Girl from the lobby!"

She smiled and playfully added, "it's eleven fifteen."

"That's good; I like girls who can tell time." The opening was made and the conversation flowed, the number was going to be easy. Soon, her body language was open and she was beginning to mirror my movements. This is where my blue belt skills went briefly into black belt, or at least a solid purple. I glanced over to Kelly and Beth and their body language had gone from interested to slightly irked. Jealous, perhaps....

I had seen my next move performed, but had never actually tried it myself, but out of curiosity and a bit of vengeance for their mockery, I began that next big move. Excusing myself from the brunette at the bar, I went back to table.

"So, did you get her number?" Beth asked.

"I haven't decided if I want it." I replied. My torso was completely turned to her, semi-blocking Kelly out of the conversation. From the reflection on the glass window, I could see both Kelly and the brunette at the bar. Both of them were glancing in my direction. I kept at it with Beth for just awhile longer.

Grabbing a cocktail napkin I asked Kelly's friend "Do you like games, how about Hangman?" and drew the following:

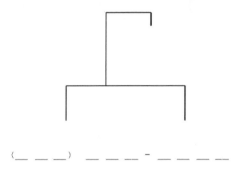

"Okay, I will go first, is there a 6?" I said with mischievous grin with a touch of smolder. (That was not technique. My grin is really smoldery, even if that's not a real word.)

She looked at me puzzled and then it hit her and then she blushed. I slid the napkin and pen over and she wrote her phone number. "That's so stupid!" she said as she giggled with her hand in front of her mouth… a body language sign of holding something in.

Kelly couldn't stand it. "What is so funny?! What is going on?!"

"Oh, I'm just hitting on your friend," I replied as I slid the digits into my pocket, got up and went back to the bar next to the brunette.

"What is going on over there? How do you know those girls?" The brunette inquired while trying to hide her competitive jealousy.

This was the move, it's the Bachelor syndrome where a girl probably doesn't like the guy, but wants to be wanted more than the other girls. Kelly, her friend and this brunette at the bar were the unknowing contestants and I was the Bachelor. The only innocent in the game was the brunette at the bar, Kelly and her friend shouldn't have teased me.

"You will have to excuse me, they got too drunk and I am going to have to do some babysitting tonight. But, I would love to follow up on the conversation we were having, can I call you?"

With the digits in hand I went back to the table and discretely showed the two naysayers. I actually had every intension to call the brunette later. I genuinely liked her.

Kelly was somewhere between happy, giddy, angry, and jealous. "You're an asshole, Mike."

For an hour more, I went back and forth between Kelly and her friend, giving arm touches, and mirroring them, paying attention to one and then the other until it was obvious that both were interested. I, on the other hand, was drunk and slightly jet-lagged and had opted to get a room at the hotel over a long cab ride. The girls wanted to check out the room before they left in a cab.

(Eight hours later.)

The next morning the three of us sat at the same table eating breakfast in the clothes from the night before.

"You're an asshole, Mike." Beth stated flatly and for no specific reason.

"You are an asshole, Mike," added Kelly. Then she swiped half of my English muffin and took a big bite.

"Hey, I just marmaladed the shit out of that toast!"

"Shut up, asshole." She mumbled through a grin full of crusty bread and apricot marmalade.

I returned to Lafayette in time for Mardi Gras season. For anyone not from Louisiana, it is difficult to get an appreciation for just how much it is engrained into the culture and just how much everything comes to a halt, and not for one day, but for two weeks.

After week one, I sent for Garrett. I needed him to experience this shit with me. The weekend before Fat Tuesday, we went down to New Orleans with my new work buddy, Stu, and another worker. The weekend wasn't pretty and by the time Fat Tuesday hit, we were spent, but felt obligated to go out and see what more could possibly happen in Lafayette that hadn't already occurred.

As we nursed a beer in a bar called The Office, I excused myself to the restroom. I made my way through the dance floor and a hand grabbed my face. Ah, crap here we go. My switch to fight flicked "ON," but just before I reacted the face attached to the body attached to the hand that grabbed me came into focus: UFC fighter Tim Credeur. He had a big toothy yet sinister grin, the look of a man who didn't mind getting punched. He yelled over the beat of the music that I should come to the gym tomorrow and help with some fighters who have cage matches coming up. In the theory of six degrees of separation, my cousin Garrett trained in college with a guy named Cameron. Cameron was the jiu-jitsu coach for former UFC Light Heavy Weight Champ Forrest Griffin on The Ultimate Fighter Show. Forrest Griffin and Tim Credeur are friends and training partners.

Even if you didn't follow all that, my point is that the world of jiu-jitsu is small, really small.

After two weeks of Mardi Gras I was in no shape to roll, but how often does a UFC fighter request your presence, especially the presence of a forty-year-old civil engineer? That was a rhetorical question. Garrett and I made our way to the gym. Tim's place had two sets of mats: an MMA area in the back and just mats out front. We waited around and the fighters showed up, but Tim was nowhere to be found. After a time it seemed the fighters had their own program, so Garrett and I, and a couple of other guys, made our way to the front mats to roll.

This was the first time Garrett and I had rolled since he had killed me in front of my kids four years earlier. Now he was in his early twenties, he was a purple belt, and he was no longer a scrawny teenager. This was not going to be a match against my brother.

Even though there was all of the above, the roll never felt like a stab at redemption. Those ego issues had long ago washed off of me. To me, it was an opportunity to show the man who had led me into this glorious divine place, that I was worthy of the knowledge he had given me. That I had learned, that I was good and that even though we were cousins, we were something more now, too, like brothers, or warriors. Shit, I'm getting all teary-eyed now.

We rolled twice, once at the beginning and once somewhere in between some other matches. I tapped everyone but Garrett. And Garrett was the only man in the room who had tapped the entire room. From the moment we started rolling, to the moment I tapped,

I was defending myself from position to position until there was no escape. I had really only felt this type of difficulty from black belts. In watching him roll with the other guys, I took note that he calculated his every next move, and anticipated theirs. From position to position, to submission, Garrett's jiu-jitsu was flawless. It was like watching art, fine art…and he was perfect in the moment.

Chapter 30

"Once more into the fray.
Into the last good fight I'll ever know.
Live and die on this day.
Live and die on this day."
—*The Grey* Joe Carnahan

Hunter Becomes the Hunted

LATE THURSDAY NIGHT IN NEW YORK CITY ON SEPTEMBER 6, 2012, TWO men wait for the sheep of the world to come staggering into the wild after a night of drinking. Their aim is to take one down and steal their possessions. They await the unknown victim near the intersection of 22nd Street and 10th Avenue. A man walks by, seemingly drunk. The sheep has left the flock and the wolves follow.

As the sheep staggers along 10th Avenue, he stops to take pictures with his phone. The two wolves pretend to look into a nearby closed shop and have discussions. The drunk continues north and the street seemingly empties of all other people. The wolves close in on the sheep. The target is not huge, 5'10", 180 pounds, shouldn't be too difficult for two large thugs.

The first wolf asks the man for a cigarette; the ploy is to close the gap.

The man replies in an accent, "I don't have it, Buddy. I don't smoke."

The wolf grabs the sheep's arm and reaches in the coat demanding the cigarette while looking for the wallet. At the same time, as if practiced, the partner circles in on the other side of the sheep.

The man is not a sheep he is a shark, and although they may be wolves, they are wolves that have jumped into deep waters. A wolf is just another meal to the shark. Before the thief could find the wallet, he was hit with a left and then a right and went down in a heap. The second mugger ran off into the night, too fast for the forty-five year old average man to chase.

The sheep/shark/drunk was Renzo Gracie of the famed Brazilian jiu-jitsu family and an expert jiu-jitsu practitioner and MMA fighter. What the two men did not realize was that not only was Renzo not drunk but he was on to them. He had baited them and they, in fact, were the hunted. Renzo tweeted the entire incident in real time as follows: [27]

@RenzoGracieBJJ: 22nd street and 10th ave right now two guys following me, can't help but have a big smile upon my face Im talking about a happy one ;-))))

@RenzoGracieBJJ: Waiting for them... Are they really thinking I'm drunk??? They have to be kidding. Hahahaha

@RenzoGracieBJJ: 25th and 10ave ;-) they are getting closer lol ;-)

@RenzoGracieBJJ: I just stopped to take a pic, they pretend they are looking at the window, can't lie... My blood runs in a different speed, man I miss Brazil.

@RenzoGracieBJJ: JiuJitsu ;-))) never leave home without it ;-)

@RenzoGracieBJJ: Please hold there for just a couple minutes ;-)

be right back.

@RenzoGracieBJJ: They are coming closer, asking for a cigaret ;-) lol can't help but have a smile in my face. I don't smoke.

@RenzoGracieBJJ: Pretend to wobble. They smile.

@RenzoGracieBJJ: My hands hurt... Can't help but look at him the other one took off running, not much of a friend. Chicken :-/ I can still see him, he looks back as he runs, no chance to catch him...

@RenzoGracieBJJ: Even though I began to try to run after him, I realize How slow I was. Fuck it :-///

Renzo returned to the mugger he had flattened and lectured him. The man hung onto his cigarette story. Anthony Miranda had asked for a cigarette before getting his foot shot when he pulled a gun on the trained guy in the car. This ploy was learned. There's generally a simple pattern amongst the underbelly of our society. Renzo kicked this unruly mugger while he continued to tweet.

@RenzoGraacieBJJ: This one asks me why did I do that, pretending to be stupid, one little kick to the ribs makes him whine and apologize, as I'm writing this.

@RenzoGracieBJJ: I ask him if he was planning to rob me, he says no. All he wanted was a cigarette, lol I can't help but have a big smile upon my face, and ..

@RenzoGracieBJJ: ...Fucking cunt cries like a bitch when the tide turns...

@RenzoGracieBJJ: I can't help but take a pic as his nose bleeds and he wines and asks why did I do that... Like he doesn't know the reason... My fucking hands hurt, hurt like hell...

Renzo continued to his car, but he couldn't help himself once he got there. He drove around until he spotted the partner, who was, as he'd imagined, looking back down the street, checking on his buddy from a safe distance. Renzo parked the car and snuck up on him. As Renzo came around the corner on foot, the mugger was standing looking the other away from his approach. Renzo dropped in a rear naked choke. This is where the jiu-jitsu waters become deep. Renzo choked him out three times. After choking him out, Renzo punched him lightly in each eye to give him a "raccoon." This is something Renzo learned in Brazil. As a way of punishment, the opponent, the bad guy, whatever you want to call him would be given a raccoon - both eyes. Gracie had said in an interview. "So after I choked him, I hit him a few times in the eye area. Nothing serious, but just to make sure that today he has two shiners." [28]

He tweeted all of that, too.

@RenzoGracieBJJ: Drove around two blocks... The other fellow disappear, I'm heading home... Angry for not finding the second one. Guess no sleeping tonight.

@RenzoGracieBJJ: I knew it ;-) yessss

@RenzoGracieBJJ: There is basic things like you don't come back to where the problem was.. You just don't, I knew he would, just going around the block would be enough...

@RenzoGracieBJJ: Dumb f%#^ I just gave him the old style Raccoon, it has been a while since the last time I did that... Choked him out 3 times...

@RenzoGracieBJJ: And before he woke up I did hit each eye socket at least twice, tomorrow he will wake up like a raccoon, and every time he woke up I was whispering at his ears..

@RenzoGracieBJJ: That's what death feels like it... Don't do that again.

@RenzoGracieBJJ: My fucking hand hurts, :-/ a lot Next time I will use only the elbows, damn I miss that feeling, sometimes I wonder if the easy life has been making me soft..

@RenzoGracieBJJ: All those years in Brazil, without knowing if I would make it home had to count for something, I can't lie I could have jumped in a cab but I could not help

@RenzoGracieBJJ: I could spot them from a mile away, walking was my option, thank you mayor Giuliani, nobody carries a gun in our beautiful state, my lucky day, their bad day...

Since the incident, some have argued that Renzo became the thug that Renzo should have run and not engaged, that the assailants could have had weapons.

Somewhere in history, the idea was put forward that your wallet, your watch, your whatever is not worth your life. While this is true, what we have done as a society with this message is effectively expressed to the wolves of the world that we will be sheep, go ahead and attack. And, over the decades, they have attacked at will. There is not a cop on every corner, so when the wolves attack, you will be alone.

Two University of Chicago economists (one being Steven Levitt, coauthor of Freakonomics) reported on the impact of LoJack in 1998. Prior to the creation of anti-theft devices and tracking devices for automobiles, theft was as much as 60% higher in major cities in the U.S. Further, a car equipped with these devices increased the arrest rate from 10% to 30%. And, even if a car didn't actually have LoJack, just the presence of an anti-theft device resulted in a dramatic change in theft activity, and, as such, society benefitted. LoJack and other tracking devices dramatically changed the behavioral patterns of car thieves. [29]

While not everyone is a shark, those that are should consider resistance and should come to the aid of others, and this long-established mantra of nonresistance ought to be ended. It doesn't work.

Chapter 31

*"It's not the daily increase but the daily decrease.
Hack away at the unessential."*
—Bruce Lee

New Church, New Shrink, NOLA BJJ!

IN SEPTEMBER 2009, I ARRIVED IN NEW ORLEANS AND STAYED WITH Aaron while I looked for a place to live. Aaron had been mobilized to New Orleans a few months prior to my arrival. After nearly a year in Lafayette, moving again had thrown off my equilibrium. Aaron and I went to the Quarter to get drunk and ended up on the patio of a bar that advertized and delivered three-for-one drinks. I was wearing a *Megaton Jiu-jitsu Competition Team t-shirt.* As we stood on the balcony, watching the Bourbon Street tourists I could feel some stares from two guys and a girl standing to my left. I said *hi* and they asked me if I trained and where I was from. They seemed curious and unimpressed by my presence at the same time.

It took a minute before Aaron recognized them from NOLA BJJ. He had started training there just a month earlier. I am always excited to talk about jiu-jitsu, but this threesome just seemed skeptical towards me. It occurred to me that I was once again going to have to prove myself and do the respect-ego dance. How had I forgotten about that?

Later in the week, Aaron drove us to NOLA BJJ, which was located in the back of Temple Gym in the Garden District of New Orleans. The building, like most in New Orleans, was built in the 1800s. It was a brick building, two stories tall and shotgun style with an arched entry. You must walk through the gym to find NOLA BJJ in the back. The mats and punching bags are partitioned off from the gym by a chain-link fence. It feels as if you're walking through normal society-office dwellers on treadmills and machines being pressed into action by their paid trainers-into a place where most won't dare to venture. For me, it was my new church, my therapist, my guide. But unlike a psychiatrist's office where the sessions are private, ours are out in the open for all to view through the web of the fencing.

Walking through the gym on the first day, I made a beeline for the fenced opening, cutting inappropriately through the gym, drawing the ire of a trainer. He puffed up and demanded we reroute around the machines. A polite request would have sufficed. I paused to stare at the guy. Had I been at Megaton's, I would have invited him to the back without pausing and began a lesson on etiquette. But Aaron steadied me, "Let it go Mike. We need this place. And Matthias is cool and doesn't need landlord issues."

I moved along thinking, man, I've despised meathead weight lifters since as long as I can remember, since high school football.

When I actually rolled, I found NOLA to be a most accepting school. Matthias didn't care about jiu-jitsu politics or things like patches from other schools. Just come and train—that was his philosophy.

Early into my training at NOLA BJJ, I sparred with a Russian purple belt. He came at me with an intensity that destroyed my soft easygoing start. I spent most of the session recovering from his jump start. Being stuck under this powerful Russian made me giggle a little on the inside; the Russian was former USSR Military and was even deployed in Afghanistan when the Russians invaded. I don't know if this rumor was the straight up truth, but it was fitting that my new school would have KGB as the counterpoint to CIA at Megaton's. And, it gave me a chuckle that they both rolled the same.

The story of NOLA BJJ is one that started with the three founding members; Matthias Meister, Marco Macera and Eddie "Doc" Lirette, who weren't exactly friends at first. Marco and Doc were born and raised in Louisiana, while Matthias had arrived from Switzerland in the 80s and then travelled the Americas before settling in New Orleans. He had come for Mardi Gras, but discovered he couldn't leave. New Orleans is a city that grabs and holds on to you.

To hear their stories is like a visit back in time, to a point where MMA was brand new to America. In 1998 Senator John McCain had declared it Human Cockfighting, and forces were out to try and ban the sport. Louisiana, being Louisiana, did not align with some other states which had banned it.

Matthias tells tales of arriving in New York and following his Jack Kerouac dream of travel by touring North America and South America on a motorcycle until eventually arriving in New Orleans for Mardi Gras. In the early 1990s he had watched Royce Gracie win the first UFCs and although Matthias had had a judo background, by 1995, he decided to take up jiu-jitsu.

Matthias was in his mid-forties when I met him, but he looks younger with his thick, gray-free dark hair and the two-day growth on his face. He doesn't look or act like a tough guy. His jiu-jitsu style fits his tall and lean frame. He rolls like the black belt that he is. My guess is that he's always rolled like a black belt. With some people you can just tell. Organizational studies courses in business school explain that successful businesses hire to their culture, meaning that they hire people of like qualities who work in a similar manner, but don't necessarily have the same beliefs. While jiu-jitsu school-hopping is frowned upon by the Brazilian culture, finding the instructor with whom you click, finding the school that feels like your culture, is more important than any jiu-jitsu politics. Matthias is this connection for me. Although he is a World Champion, it's his philosophy, his demeanor on the mat, his care-free attitude towards rolling with his students that all align with how I want to be. Win or lose, he has a smile on his face.

Marco was in his early thirties, and was about six feet tall and weighed in around two hundred pounds. Over beers one day, Marco told of a time when he'd fight on the weekends at a local bar for a few hundred bucks. He was only seventeen at the time. The bar owner would set up the fights, which at times included the fighters mixing it up with tough guy patrons, or whatever. Marco had said that the tables were too close to the ring and guys would literally fly from ring-to-table frequently. Rolling with Marco is like rolling with the elite grapplers from the best schools from around the country. He has a flow, he knows your move before you do, mid-move he greets you pleasantly, and then slams the door in your face. His style is varied yet elegant, but you can't quite pin it down.

Contrasting Marco is Doc. Doc was a fairly successful Tough Man contestant in the 1990s. Doc likes to mix it up and for all of his brilliance and prestige as a doctor; he has been known to get into trouble at some of the local watering holes. As we were born on the same day and year, I refer to him my evil twin. A brown belt from Phoenix who I know from the tournament circuit recently joined NOLA BJJ and posted on Facebook that there is not a position with Doc Eddie that does not involve pain. It's like Doc took his knowledge of human anatomy and combined it with jiu-jitsu and medieval torture techniques, and that's how he rolls. When rolling with him, you immediately know where the weakness in your game is because your central nervous system tells you. On the other hand, when teaching, he does very well at breaking the position into parts and simplifying the move.

As Matthias was learning jiu-jitsu at one school, Marco and Doc were at another. But then the two schools shut down, so in spite of not really liking each other the three of them came together and opened up NOLA BJJ.

New Orleans is the birthplace of jazz: a few guys knew a couple of notes—improvised the rest—and out of it an entire genre of music was created and a city shaped itself around that. That probably best describes the creation of jiu-jitsu in New Orleans, too. One day a Brazilian jiu-jitsu black belt named Leo showed up from Brazil and observed the school. He then offered to roll with them. Their eyes were opened. Leo stayed on and began the process of giving belts and instructing.

Although, Matthias described it best when he said to me, "New Orleans jiu-jitsu and MMA history began in the mid-nineties with a bunch of martial arts enthusiasts and fans of the UFC deciding to venture out into the land of BJJ with the limited grappling skills they had gained thru traditional grappling arts like judo, jiu-jitsu and wrestling. These folks would meet three times a week to exchange this limited knowledge with like-minded people. The sport found a place in New Orleans, but it was still unrefined and rough around the edges. A core group of these original Louisiana grapplers kept at it until New Orleans got its first verified black belt instructor straight out of Brazil (Leo Xavier). That would become the official incarnation of NOLA BJJ formed on the foundation of a rag tag group of enthusiasts from different walks of life."

In 2005, Hurricane Katrina destroyed the building their jiu-jitsu school was in but it did not shut down practices. They started training out of Doc Eddie's garage and eventually re-opened at the current location in the Garden District.

Shortly after my arrival in 2009, NOLA BJJ became a Gracie Barra affiliate under Rafael Ellwanger. However, Louisiana is not the land of conformists, and by 2012 the school once again became independent and just NOLA BJJ.

Standing on the balcony overlooking the Quarter drinking my ninth three-for-one beer, pondering the three people to my left, I could not have possibly known all of this history. This tight knit community of rag-tag enthusiasts would of course look at me unimpressed and with skepticism. Eventually, all three would accept me into the group. Well, after a few friendly black eyes were exchanged anyway.

Chapter 32

"Never never never give up!"
—Winston Churchill

Not a Victim

On January 19, 2013, an off-duty, US Navy sailor took her 24-hour shore leave in Dubai by going to the Mall of Emirates and a supermarket. After shopping, the twenty-eight-year old attempted to hail a cab when a bus pulled up next to her. Opting for the bus ride, she climbed on and went to the back. After a short time, it became apparent that the bus was not on the correct route.

The sailor asked the driver about the route and he told her not to worry. Ten minutes later the driver parked in a deserted area adjacent to other vacant buses, went to the back and began tearing the sailor's clothes off and attempted to rape her. In court testimony, the sailor recounted, "I resisted him to the best of my ability, but he touched me all over. He touched my breasts and bit me everywhere…the more I resisted, the harder he bit me." Once the assailant pulled a knife, she stopped resisting. However, when the opportunity presented itself, she acted, knocking the knife from the assailant's hand, breaking the blade and ultimately forcing him to the ground where she applied a submission hold. "For fear of him cutting me I did what he asked, but when he attempted to fondle my breasts again, I saw my chance. I knocked the knife from his hand, and had him in a stranglehold between my thighs."[30]

The sailor left the bus and returned to port where she reported the incident to her superiors. Forensics found her blood on the bus and the assailant drunk at his home the next day. He was arrested and charged.[31]

Chapter 33

"If you think, you're late.
If you're late, you muscle.
If you muscle, you get tired.
If you tire, you die."
—Saulo Ribeiro

Rick and Matt

ONE NIGHT AARON INVITED ME TO DINNER WITH HIM AND A GUY HE worked with in Houston named Rick. Rick was in his early thirties, a high intensity individual, about six feet tall and thirty pounds overweight. Rick had been on the Katrina disaster early on along with a guy named Matt. Matt was not a very big guy. And Matt was soft spoken, even shy in nature. Matt was the polar opposite of Rick. Aaron and I started discussing jiu-jitsu. Rick, being of a high intensity nature, was interested and had twelve things to add to the conversation that had nothing to do with the price of tea in China. Contrastingly, Matt could tell you every UFC fighter and their stats. He was a regular walking Sherdog.com, but while he knew the fighters and the moves, he had no idea about the sport.

We kept at them to come join us and train. In the spring of 2010, they finally did. Both had sat at a desk in New Orleans for so many years that walking to the car was considered a cardiovascular activity. I didn't give Matt more than a week. Rick would stick with it, though. I knew his ego wouldn't give him any other choice.

Matthias recalls how horrible Rick was when doing private lessons. I remember him saying that some guys would never be very good at jiu-jitsu; some aren't so teachable.

One day before class and after a few months of training, Rick asked me to roll with him. I accepted. We high-fived and began. I was trying to give him an energy and effort that matched his skill, not crush him. But at a certain point, I just quit using my arms. I tucked both of my hands into my belt and choked him out several times using just my legs via triangle chokes.

In order to keep my forty-year-old body going, I worked out twice a day and did jiu-jitsu two to three times per week. If I trained more than that, I started to get injuries. I cautioned Rick that he might be training too hard after rolling with him. He was training jiu-jitsu everyday and following it up with kickboxing. It wasn't long before Rick messed up his neck, but that didn't stop him. Nothing stopped him. His pudgy frame began to harden and take shape. The morphing had begun. This metamorphosis was not only happening with his body but his spirit as well. His intensity was still there, but he was calmer, less of a know-it-all. Jiu-jitsu was the Ritalin Rick needed.

One weekend after Rick had gotten his blue belt, his wife came to town. We were at a bar and she was commenting on what a nerd Rick was, which was and is true. (The best jiu-jitsu fighters are nerds.) As Rick went to the bar to get another round, I told her to look at him.

His chiseled back was evident through his T-shirt. I said, "You may not realize this, but he is a killer. Look around this bar, there is not a man in this bar that Rick could not absolutely dismantle." It was true, but it didn't seem like she could get her head around it. Maybe later she'd get her legs around her husband, thanks to that comment.

Rick eventually moved back to San Diego and began training at Saulo Ribeiro's. He then began a jiu-jitsu journey that made mine look like summer camp. He started a blog and has traveled to Brazil for a Saulo camp capped off with a tournament. He's also attended just about every tournament he could find. This summer he received his purple belt from Saulo. Shortly after, he came back to New Orleans for a brief stay. We rolled, he nearly caught me, I fought out and then nearly caught him and he fought out. We battled and battled and after twenty minutes the only thing that was indisputable was that I could no longer tap him with just my legs.

Early on, I had given Rick my copy of Saulo Ribeiro's book University of Jiu-jitsu. He took the book and eventually put instructions on the inside cover alongside each of our names. The instructions were that the book was to be given to new promising students and when they had gotten good enough, they needed to sign the book and pass it on to another promising student. For him, that student was Matt.

As I mentioned Matt is small. He's Tom Cruise small minus the muscley build. And Matt is not an aggressive man; not a deliberate man. Let me tell you there is nothing more satisfying than seeing a guy of Matt's stature become empowered by jiu-jitsu. While Matt did not hit the sport with the intensity of Rick, despite the knowledge that he'd be the smallest guy on the mats, he has trained consistently several times per week and has always competed regularly.

One day, I saw Matt stuck under a two hundred and thirty pound white belt that had clearly chosen Matt to roll with based purely on his stature. Matt was defending per Saulo's book, one hand in his collar. He looked comfortable, not stressed, not worried. Two hundred and thirty pounds of sweaty man trying to kill him and he looked like he could have been reading a book or watching TV! That was impressive. Jiu-jitsu had morphed Matt as well. It was visible in the thickness of his neck, the shape of his back, in the confidence of his walk and even the clothes he now wore.

I was at work one day when a fellow contractor and architect named Susan said to me, "I don't know what kind of club jiu-jitsu is, but I can see the difference—a confidence and a swagger in the guys you have gotten to join."

Chapter 34

"Success is not final; failure is not fatal:
It is the courage to continue that counts."
—Winston Churchill

The March toward Brown

SHORTLY AFTER RICK HAD RECEIVED HIS BLUE BELT, A SMALL GRACIE BARRA tournament took place in New Orleans. I decided to do it. I felt a bit conflicted, though, because in my mind I was a Megaton student, but I was also a NOLA BJJ student, and as they were a new Gracie Barra school, I wanted them well represented. So I donned my Gracie Barra gi from NOLA BJJ and entered the tournament. Because the tournament was small, my weight bracket was combined to include everyone from two hundred and seven pounds on up. And there were no age brackets. Each match was seven minutes.

For my first match there was nothing but confidence pumping through my veins. I don't know why, that's just the way it was. I wanted to show my teammates that Tournament Mike was in the house; He's the guy who competes well. My opponent shot a single leg, I stuffed it and began dismantling him with side control, then to mount, then I went into technical mount, to bow and arrow choke attempt, to back, to rear naked choke attempt. The points and positions were adding up quickly. He managed to stand up with me on his back. I thought about the clock, heard "Thirty seconds!" and let him go. I stayed away from him until twenty seconds were left and then he managed to pull guard. I grabbed his lapels, shoved them into his armpits and held on for the final seconds. But my opponent had other plans. He broke free of the grip of my left hand, slid my arm to his shoulder and caught a straight arm bar with less than ten seconds. Mentally, I refused to tap, then a very distinct crunch and pop resounded from my arm. The pain in my elbow came fast, hard and sharp. I tapped with precisely one second left.

I know I am supposed to care-feel disappointment, anger, sadness, etc. Still I don't. It's what I dig about jiu-jitsu, what I find so bitchin' (bringing this word back). This man hung in there, didn't quit, waited for my mistake and his moment, and caught me. Years later I sat with that very guy's son in the bleachers at the Master Seniors Tournament in Long Beach. While this kid did exactly the same thing to one opponent and then almost again to a guy from Saulo's school that Rick had said was a monster.

I was ingrained at my new school, but I felt my loyalties belonged with Megaton. I also knew that if I ever wanted to progress, I needed someone to evaluate me. One weekend while I was home, I asked Megaton what I should do. He recommended having the school I was training with evaluate both myself and Aaron. I went back to Matthias and asked him what he'd like to see from me, not a guarantee of a completion of the journey to brown belt, just to point me in the upward direction. Matthias, Doc and I had signed up for the Pan Americans, so he told me to win the Pan Ams and he would give me my brown belt, or continue to come two to three times a week and he would consider it at the December promotions—which were about nine months away. With my new goal in place, I settled into NOLA BJJ.

One day Matthias asked me to lead the warm ups. Memories of being a white belt with Megaton yelling at and driving us during training flooded me. I asked Matthias if I could change things up. He agreed. And in I came with the one minute circuit drill that I learned by Megaton: Pull guard on a standing opponent and do sit ups while keeping them in guard, then leap frog over and dive through the legs, then bridal carry your partner up and down the mat, then wheel barrel your partner up and down the mat and the like.

When we were done, the class was exhausted. It felt good to see brand new students wondering what they had just walked into, and it was pretty stimulating to see old students, and many former wrestlers, enjoying that throwback to high school or college, being pushed to the limit. I took over this part of class on days I trained. I would look over the class and if I spotted a student who was too aggressive, the warm up would be very hard. The goal was to take the fight out of him, take his muscle away and make him use technique. I was becoming more and more a member of NOLA BJJ.

Aaron was continuing his journey as well. Every Tuesday and Thursday, he and I would train, and afterwards we'd go across the street to NY Pizza for a slice and a beer. It was a nice motivator on days

I was not feeling it. One day we asked Matthias to join us. Now on most Tuesdays and Thursdays a good portion of the team can be found there after class. It's good to meet up with these people outside of class and get to know them all on another level. I didn't meet any felons at my new school, which would have been interesting. You learn a lot about how a person acts initially on the mats when you discover what life they're stepping out of to study jiu-jitsu.

As Aaron continued his jiu-jitsu journey, he had a few more financial hurdles to leap over, along with some injuries, so there were more starts and stops. But having rolled with him for years, I knew how naturally good he was at the sport. I can honestly say that Aaron has helped me overcome my doubts when shooting omaplatas (shoulder lock) and arm bars. Early on in New Orleans, Matthias had a Free For All Mini Tournament (think gang fight) with all of the blue and white belts. The last man standing got a free T-shirt. Aaron was that man.

There was a midyear belt promotion and Aaron was passed over for purple belt. He was disappointed, I was disappointed. The three black belts wanted to see Aaron show up more often, which is why they hesitated. They were not wrong. The purple people eater returned. After the belt promotion, several of us made our way to a bar called Evangeline's. The bar was across town in an area in the boundary between shotgun homes and warehouses. It was a speakeasy that required an invitation to enter. By that I mean you had to be identified by the bartender and then get officially buzzed in. As we celebrated, Aaron began to pontificate—like I had done when I was passed over—that if he had to prove himself, he was hunting purples. En vino veritas, but this special brand of pontification needed an intervention. It was the wrong audience. I let my drunk friend prattle on, as he seemed like he was more about rambling and less about proving himself that night, while I basically begged Matthias to give him the belt. I told him of Aaron's journey and how I thought he was worthy. He had the skills. He'd put in the time—it was just all over the place—Phoenix, Virginia, Houston, New Orleans so no one saw him through this whole journey, no one but me. For all of Aaron's bravado, he promptly tore his shoulder. He tried to train, but couldn't. Several months later Matthias asked me to make sure Aaron was at class. I gave Aaron some bullshit about coming to class for the website picture, so that he would dress out in spite of not being able to roll.

Aaron showed.

Matthias stated eloquently upon seeing my man, "There are many ways to get to purple belt. One way is to come to class and train, another way is to win tournaments, another way is to bribe the instructor, another way is get drunk and threaten to beat all of the purple belts in the world and yet another way is to have your best friend plead your case. Congratulations, Aaron."

Chapter 35

"...I am at peace, I am your friend, and I can destroy you."
—Joey Hernandez, Photographer

Yoked

RICK HAD RETURNED HOME TO SAN DIEGO AFTER WORKING A YEAR IN New Orleans. Joey Hernandez wrote the above quote about Rick upon seeing the positive transformation jiu-jitsu had made upon his old high school friend.

On September 11, 2012, Rick returned to his house in San Diego after running an errand. By this time he had de-mobilized from working in New Orleans. Rick's house was a disaster as it was in mid-remodel. He was prepared for that. What he wasn't banking on when he pulled up to his home was seeing a strange guy walking out of his backyard with his new power saw. This dude, who looked to be in his thirties, was yoked (that's Rick's term for muscular), and he had the obligatory tats adorning muscled-up arms, plus he was sporting the gangster teardrop below his right eye as an added don't-fuck-with-me warning. He legitimately looked like he could be in construction in between jail stays, but he wasn't working on Rick's house.

Rick was pissed. He hopped out of his car with the intent of subduing this thief and sending him back to jail.

Rick said that when the guy saw him, he gave him a look that said, "What are you gonna do about it?" and that's when Rick charged him. In recalling the event, Rick said, "I was surprised by how angry I got initially. I felt violated that someone would dare come on my property and try to steal something. But by the time I had my hands on him I started to calm down. I was pleased at how clearly I was thinking before the take down. I pinned him to the garage door, dropped him with a leg trip by adjusting my hips and feet to trip him, but controlled his fall, so neither of us got hurt. And I ended up in a dominant top position from that. Wish it were that easy in competition."

Rick recollected that he was most concerned about wrist control, in case the thief had a weapon. So when he took him down and secured the wrists, he went into a fierce knee on belly, causing the thief to shit himself. "The knee on belly was pure intimidation. I could tell he was having trouble breathing and saw deep fear in his eyes. He tried to roll over by twisting his upper body. He had no clue how to bump, making my job extra easy. when I finally got him to calm down and look me in the eyes, I told him my wife and kid are home sick and asked what most husbands would do to him at that moment. He started begging me to not hurt him. Said he has a family too and he's just trying to provide for them. I said I wasn't going to hurt him, but that he's very lucky because had it been someone else he could have had a very bad day. He apologized profusely and started bawling. When I let him up he said, 'God bless you, I'm so sorry' and took off running for his truck parked across the street. I really don't think I'm going to see him again."

Then Rick jokingly added that at no point did he ever think, "Hmm...should I pull guard?" A frequent criticism of jiu-jitsu is that it doesn't work on the street and that all jiu-jitsu guys fight from their back. But Rick proved to himself, and any other regular guy who train that it does work on the street, and jiu-jitsu works even when you don't have time to think your next move through.

As Rick told me the story over a few beers at a hotel in San Diego, I couldn't help but reflect on the guy who couldn't beat a man without arms less than two years earlier.

Who knows what that guy would have done? Maybe he would have pulled a tire iron or golf club out of his car and began beating the saw thief. Or gotten beat up himself. Or worse yet-retreated into the house feeling the loss of not just the saw, but of his manhood, too. This guy, this guy who stopped the yoked perp using an appropriate combination of force and mercy, this guy Aaron and I helped to create; this guy was perfect in the moment.

Chapter 36

"Tomorrow is the most important thing in life.
Comes into us at midnight very clean.
It's perfect when it arrives and puts itself in our hands.
It hopes we've learned something from yesterday."
—John Wayne

Pantastic

In the spring of 2011, I decided to take Matthias up on his offer and go win myself a brown belt. Matthias, Doc, a guy named Collin, who was a brown belt and I all signed up for the Pan Americans at UC Irvine. As I mentioned earlier, I was conflicted by teams. This issue was a continuation of the economic woes of the country. If the economy had not run me off to Louisiana, this would not be an issue. I thought about it and my logic was simple. The purple belt was given to me by Megaton so I would sign up under the Megaton flag. Also, my Megaton, gi was about two pounds lighter in weight than my Gracie Barra NOLA BJJ gi. I'd be a liar if I didn't state the whole truth here.

Matthias and I actually trained pretty hard for the tournament, conditioning, extra rounds, long rounds, etc. I am not sure about Doc because he usually trains in the afternoon, but Matthias and I had made serious preparations.

Doc booked us a nice place on the ocean in Orange County. He and Matthias flew out together. As Gracie Barra school representatives, they had to attend a series of mandatory meetings. Collin flew out separately with his girlfriend and made other arrangements. I flew out to Phoenix a week before and then drove out and met up with them. I liked being able to sweat off a few pounds in the desert while driving to the tournament. It was practically a ritual at this point.

I arrived and met up with Doc and Matthias. We walked about the beach a bit, and then Collin and his girlfriend joined us at a restaurant at the end of the pier. I nibbled on some of the others' plates, but my weight was close and I didn't want to risk it. I enjoyed the company, the sunset and one beer. When you can only have one beer, it is the best beer.

The next day the three of us headed to the gym for the tournament. Doc performed well, beating his first opponent. But his match had taken a lot of hand strength and his grips were shot. He lost a grueling second match. Matthias went up against a feisty Brazilian and lost on points. He was disappointed.

I entered the bullpen and began the ritual of warming up. The bullpen is its own experience. You try to get your body warmed up among the hundred or so contestants while trying to figure out who is in your bracket. Sometimes it's easy to tell, sometimes you know the opponent, sometimes it's not easy to tell. Warming up consists of a lot of jumping around as there is not much room to do more. When your name is called, you squeeze through the crowd of fighters, show your ID, get weighed, get your gi checked and then follow an usher to your mat with your opponent. Once arriving to your mat you have to wait for the prior match to finish. Doc and Matthias were at the mat. They were waiting to watch me.

My opponent and I slapped hands and the match was on. He immediately shot for my legs. I must have looked like an easy take down. This guy did get fairly deep as I began my sprawl. I heard Doc yell, "Hump the mat!" I was trying to sprawl when I heard him add, "Simpson! Take your dick and stick it into the mat!" I drove my hips harder into the mat and began to look for a Darce choke. My opponent, feeling the choke beginning to be set up, drove forward forcing us off the mat. The referee restarted us in a standing position.

Upon the restart, he attempted another takedown, but his balance was off and I jumped on it driving him onto his ass and forcing him to pull guard. I began to break his guard open, but I felt my balance off, so I retreated. Doc and Matthias were yelling for me to drive the knee through harder. It was too late, he had closed his guard and was holding on tight for the final moments. The match ended. The ref gave my opponent the zero to zero decision. Neither of us had scored any points or advantage points, so the referee picked the winner. Later that night over beers, Doc was explaining to me that driving that knee more aggressively would have been the win. A week later in practice rolls, I tried Doc's suggestion. He was right, it would have worked.

What I remember most from that trip was Doc and Matthias in my corner. You see, my opponent was a Gracie Barra student from some other city. His coaches were looking at my Megaton gi and with my coaches wearing Gracie Barra T-shirts, they were irritated. My coaches were backing me regardless of jiu-jitsu politics. They were my friends and I felt more than ever a part of the NOLA BJJ team. Regardless, that was a big loss. There wasn't going to be an early brown belt for me. Matthias slapped me on the back and reminded me that the Phoenix Open was just around the corner.

Chapter 37

"Do not pray for easy lives. Pray to be stronger men."
—John Kennedy

Hotel Choke Out

A LITTLE BEFORE MIDNIGHT ON WEDNESDAY NOVEMBER 11, 2011, AN unassuming male in his thirties walked into The Comfort Inn near Universal Studios in Los Angeles. He was carrying a backpack over one shoulder and sporting a beanie cap, looking more hippie than gangster. But within a couple minutes he had made his way behind the counter, and he was brandishing a handgun and demanding money.[32]

Two guys, also in their thirties, Brent Alvarez and Billy Denny, had driven down from Oregon on a jiu-jitsu road trip. Brent was a purple belt and Billy was a blue belt. They were in town for the IBJJF Worlds No-Gi Jiu-jitsu Tournament. Brent and Billy were staying at The Comfort Inn. They had just left the well-known 10th Planet Jiu-jitsu School after training and had checked into the hotel moments before the armed robber had appeared. Exhausted from the road trip and from rolling at 10th Planet, they cruised directly up to their room, but only to discover that the electronic keys weren't working.

Unbeknownst to this robber, he was on an intersecting path with

Brent Alvarez and Billy Denny. And this path was about to change his plan and his life forever.

As Brent and Billy exited the elevator at 11:33 P.M. in pursuit of new key cards, the robber came out from behind the counter and bumped squarely into the duo. The clerk started yelling that he had just been robbed at gunpoint.[33] The robber may as well have walked straight into a pair of hungry lions.

As the guy grabbed his gun again, Brent and Billy immediately reached for wrist control. Within seconds the hand with the gun was immobilized and the gun was out of his possession. The duo then slowly and methodically sucked the fight right out of the assailant until finally the man had no defenses left in him at all. He was a puddle, spent, flaccid, shapeless within the jiu-jitsu holds being placed on him. He was still conscious, but he was on the ground and he wasn't going anywhere. Brent used verbal reasoning skills to calm the robber down, as well. And Billy finished with a body lock along with a rear naked choke. The body lock restricted breathing. Billy never choked the robber out, though. Later, they confessed it probably would have been safer just to knock him out. But that was the jiu-jitsu way, to restrain and reason. So that took five minutes.

At approximately 11:44 P.M., the police arrived, nearly eleven minutes after the initial confrontation. The police were not slow in responding; the robbery and scuffle prevented anyone from calling them. But the hotel clerk plus Brent and Billy were alone until they got there.

In interviews, both Brent and Billy exuded a certain compassion for the robber, stating that the entire time they were restraining him he was begging to be let go so that he could see his daughter one last time. And both implied that they had sensed that he was a man who believed that he had just run out of options.

Nevertheless, he was booked and faced seven years for suspicion of armed robbery.

Chapter 38

"The race is not to the swift,
Nor the battle to the strong,
Neither yet bread to the wise,
Nor yet riches to men of understanding,
Nor yet favor to men of skill;
But time and chance happen to them all."
—Ecclesiastes 9:11

Brown Belt

WHEN I WAS A WHITE BELT, MEGATON LEFT TOWN FOR A STRETCH AND had his brown belt cousin from the Reunion Islands fill in for him at the school. His private lesson prices were very reasonable, so I purchased about ten from him. I was mesmerized by his skill and talent. And, while I knew I was going to keep at this until black belt status had been attained, the skill level that he possessed as a brown belt seemed inconceivable. I couldn't get my head around being this good some day. And yet here in New Orleans, in the spring of 2011, nearly eight years after starting this adventure, I was nearly a brown belt. I could now see what he saw. And, while this view was not from the peak of the mountain, I could see plenty nonetheless. For this reason, achieving brown belt status meant so much.

Over time, NOLA BJJ managed to mirror Megaton's school in Phoenix in that I was beginning to feel like I was a part of the pack. I grew close with the group of people with whom I rolled, and I trusted them that I would go home generally uninjured. The new tightly knit group of fellow purple belts included the likes of characters named Doc Ken, Gavin, Charlie and Alex. I even became friends with the girl from the balcony in the French Quarter on my first night in New Orleans, a brown belt named Caroline. Because of my commitment to travel back to Phoenix most weekends, my ability to hit the tournament circuit with these people, like I had done before at Megaton's, was basically inhibited. However, seeing them during the week gave me a smile. Our friendships definitely turned New Orleans into a place I could start calling home, too.

Matthias offered me another shot at brown belt. All I had to do was win The Phoenix Open. This was his second offer to get promoted by way of the tournament circuit and I took him up on it. So, in the spring of 2011 I took some time off work and signed up for The Phoenix Open. I figured there would be old Megaton friends there and it would be a good time, too. Actually it's always a good time. I'm that guy, the one who usually has a good time. And if I'm not having one, I change the view. That part's always been simple.

By the time the tournament was a go, there was only one guy in my bracket, but I had signed up for the open weight class as well, which was fairly full. My weight bracket opponent was a no-show which left my matches in the open weight class.

Savannah, my daughter showed up to watch. None of my Megaton friends were there and by the time my match was up, my corner consisted of just Savannah. I liked that she was there, only she was a teenager now, not the little girl who had sat cross legged in my championship match years ago screaming, "Go, Daddy, go!"

My opponent was taller than I was, but he was about ten pounds lighter. When I grabbed his lapel I could feel his energy was light so I pressed for the take down. I shot, he sprawled, I recovered standing, then pressed forward. My momentum took him off the mat. This process continued several times. I was waiting for the ref to warn him for going off the mat, but it never came. Based on the rules, and the fact that his retreat from the mat had happened six times, he should have been disqualified. I relented and pulled guard. His tall frame that had sprawled well also served him in stuffing several of my sweep attempts. Late in the match, out of habit from rolling in class, I went to half guard, which gave him an advantage point. He stuffed my half guard attempts. Pulling the position was stupid on my part, but as the saying goes, you play like you practice. I lost because of this mistake. I stayed and watched him get disqualified for leaving the mat too many times in his second match. Oh, sweet irony.

I certainly don't hang onto my losses, but I do consider them for next time. Where did I fail? What move could have ensured a win? What was my fatal flaw in that particular match? What was my opponent's weakness? What was his strength? How did I not detect his strengths and take advantage of his weaknesses sooner? And, once all this information is gathered, how can I best use it to prevent my next loss? After analyzing all that, I realized that my path to brown belt, much like my path through life, has no short cuts. I went back and continued training two to three times each week knowing that the brown belt would require more time on the mat.

A few weeks before the promotions, Doc Eddie told me that since I had never submitted him, he wasn't sure about the promotion. After class, I pull him aside to roll. I brought my A game. Catching him with a flower sweep, I went to set an arm triangle. He eventually skated out of it and we battled on. I then set up an arm bar, I thought it was tight, it was tight until his knee came down on me. With blood dripping out of my nose, we ended it. Still no submission on Doc Eddie.

On December 3, 2011, Professors Matthias, Doc Eddie, Marco and Rafael presented Gavin, Doc Ken, Alex and me our brown belts. I got that goddamned belt after all.

Purple Belt Accomplishments:

Eight Years ✓✓✓✓✓✓✓

Ass Kicked ✓

Humbled ✓

Slew of New Friends ✓

Soul Saved ✓

Mind Right ✓

3 Tournaments ✓✓✓

0 Wins ✿

4 Losses ✿✿✿✿

1 Gold Medal ✿

3 Bronze Medals ✿✿✿

(these medals were won without beating an opponent, thus ✿)

Black Eyes ✓

Knee Surgery (left) ✓

Self-esteem ✓

Nearly 5,000 hours of jiu-jitsu ✓

Six Pack Abs for my Girlfriend ✍

Girlfriend ✓

215 Pounds ✓

110 degree trip through the desert to lose two pounds ✓

Chapter 39

"The mind is weak. The body is strong."
—Uncle John Oeltman

Twenty Eight Minutes

As a chubby kid in the 80's trying to run and train alongside my uncle, he would run around me not allowing me to stop by telling me, "Mike, the mind is weak. The body is strong. The mind wants to give up, but the body will fight for life long after the mind has left." He had a way of putting it not like an asshole coach, but like he was molding me into a warrior, like gladiator out of a movie, or like Yoda.

This is a parable of the hardening of the mind.

Out of the group of former purple belts at NOLA BJJ, I have spent the most time rolling with Doc Ken. I have spent the most time outside of class with this character as well. He is about a year younger than I am. He's a nice-sized dude who's handsome and chicks dig him. Ken's jiu-jitsu style is strong with technique. You can't give him an inch, and I've never tried anything new on him until I've studied and perfected it with others. I've always considered Ken to be a slightly better opponent than I am, but I would never relent over this feeling, which brings me to one of the best rolls I have ever had.

Matthias had asked Ken and me to run the class because he had to scram early. When it came time to roll, Ken came up with the idea that we should eliminate the time limit and grapple until you get submitted or submit your partner. We had an odd number of people, so when someone got submitted, they would replace that person, that's how we took care of that. My first roll was with a blue belt. He was much smaller than me, so I was giving him lighter energy when he shot for a heel hook. The move was unexpected. I spent a minute slowly releasing myself from the position and then submitted him quickly.

The next guy up was Doc Ken....

I looked at the clock, twenty-five minutes left in class...

Crap, this is going to be grueling.

We began to roll.

After some time, Ken had passed my guard and was controlling well. I glanced at the clock, twenty minutes... *Alright, quit looking at the clock, Fucker! You let him pass, you put yourself here. This is your goddamned punishment! Take your punishment! Your mind is weak, your body is strong!* Having a two hundred and ten pound brown belt in a dominate control is not ideal, especially when he is well acquainted with all of your tricks, knows what your poison is and can anticipate when you'll deliver it.

Ken was bringing the heat. He had my back and was throwing choke attempts from all angles.

Years earlier, while watching an episode of the Ultimate Fighter, a coach, Matt Serra was yelling at his fighter who was in a similar spot.

"Hand fight! Hand fight! This fight right now comes down to a hand fight!" Remember, it's the simple things like "Hand fight!" and "If you can breathe you can fight!" that keep you going.

As Ken poured on his choke attempts, "Hand Fight!" shot through my mind and so that's what I did. After a time, I glanced at the clock, not out of looking for relief this time, but out of curiosity. Fifteen minutes had passed and the thought struck me that Ken may actually mentally break if I continue to defeat his attacks. I continued to work out of the spot I was in and with five minutes until the end of class I had made my way back into his guard. Class ended. We did not stop. At about twenty eight minutes into the roll, I caught him in my bread and butter submission, an arm triangle.

Although Ken was my actual, physical opponent, my real opponent was me. The only way out was to quit or submit and I was in a bad spot with a superior opponent. I did not quit, and on that day my mind happened to be as strong as my body.

Chapter 40

"A black belt only covers two inches of your ass.
You have to cover the rest."
—Royce Gracie

Bullies and Friends

The kids' class at NOLA BJJ was before the adult class. I loved watching them roll. Kids are entirely uninhibited. When I was a white belt, I learned spider guard by watching Megaton's daughter, McKenzie, who was twelve at the time. I've arrived early many times just to watch them.

One day in New Orleans, this kid who was about fourteen showed up. He was not coordinated, not athletic, he was clumsy and a bit doughy. Slowly but surely he started training, and kept at it. The kid kept showing up even though he didn't seem to be progressing too quickly. Matthias started letting him go to the adult class as well. And he was just as horrible there. He had even less coordination. I can't explain why. I probably just missed my own kids, but I began to work with him. He was goofy, nerdy on top of everything else. There's no way this kid was popular. One day in the middle of class, he turned to me straight and plain and said, "I'm getting bullied at school." It didn't surprise me that he was getting bullied. It did surprise me that he said it out loud.

That was a clear cry for help. I thought about the advice I would give my own son. After class I pulled him aside and found out that some jock-type and his minions were the bullies. And because he had worked his ass off to steer clear of these guys, they were now hunting him. He said his parents knew about it, which was the reason they had signed him up for jiu-jitsu.

My first thought was to go scare the shit out of them myself, but that wouldn't do any good in the long run. So I thought about it some more and then drafted a plan:

1) Tell the principal what's going on. Give the people in charge some time to correct the problem.
2) Do not tell the bully or any of the kids at school about jiu-jitsu. If a fight should ensue, that would be a nice surprise. Plus mentioning jiu-jitsu might actually provoke more harassment.
3) If #1 doesn't work, tell the kid that there's going to be a real, scheduled fight.

He looked at me with deep concern.

I knew he was afraid of a fight for the same reason we all are: pain and trouble. He didn't want to get hurt, and he didn't want to be in trouble. The problem is that the emotional scars he was taking on would impact him well into his adult life.

Finally I reasoned, "Look, you can have one fight and never have to deal with this again. Or you can continue to deal with this daily." He didn't seem sold, so I kept going. "You don't even have to win the fight. They will move on to easier targets just because you stood up for yourself. Trust me on this."

He still didn't seem sold.

"Hey, have you ever smashed into something and gotten a bloody nose?" I asked.

"…Yeah."

"That's all this is. It's a bloody nose and all your bully troubles will be behind you."

Next, I addressed the psychology of being in trouble for fighting. "You are going to the principal for help. If he fails you, it is up to you to save yourself. I don't care if you get in trouble by a person who fails you and neither should you."

The kid actually smiled and showed some relief.

We started meeting before every class to work on a straight punch and some defensive moves against the standard bully arsenal of head-locks. Then some other upper belts worked with him when I went away on rotation. Upon my return a few weeks later, I noticed that this uncoordinated, soft and passive kid was walking around with some swagger. I asked Matthias if I was seeing things, and Matthias said that the kid was definitely rolling better and seemed more confident.

When I asked the kid how the meeting at school went he said that he never spoke with the principal. But as it turns out the principal spoke with him. Apparently one of the minions threatened the kid, so the kid challenged him to a fight. That's one way to go. He skipped the first two steps in my plan and went straight to the fight. Anyway, both the kid and the bully ended up getting their asses chewed in the principal's office about the consequences of fighting. The bullying stopped altogether after that.

I helped a former employee of mine named Jason get a position in New Orleans. It was good to have an old friend around. Jason is about a decade younger than me. We used to wakeboard and water-ski together, that's how we propelled our work relationship into a friendship. He regularly participated in Ironman Triathlons; the guy was in great shape. One night we were down at the French Quarter and this guy started harassing us, nothing crazy, just your standard crazy. As always, nothing came of it but I watched Jason get puffed up, in the way of the untrained. That night I started urging him to seriously take up jiu-jitsu.

After several months of prodding, he finally accompanied me to a jiu-jitsu class. It was shortly thereafter that I left for rotation. When I got back to the city and back to class, I went in early as I had been doing and there was Jason, my one hundred and eighty pound Ironman tough guy friend getting handled by the kid. This is when I knew the kid would be fine. Ironically, I thought the same for Jason. His transformation had begun, too. Jiu-jitsu was breaking him down. And one day in the near future I was looking forward to watching it build him back up.

From the swagger that materializes out of nowhere, which seems to be a standard trait everyone takes on, to the calm inner confidence that develops, jiu-jitsu is life-changing. Introducing others to this sport, bringing them into the light and witnessing this change truly makes all the time on the mat worth it.

Chapter 41

"I will prepare and some day my chance will come."
—Abraham Lincoln

Frequent Flyer Miles

ON FRIDAY FEBRUARY 3, 2012 I FLEW TO RENO TO MEET UP WITH MY college buddies, Joe and Nate, for Super Bowl Sunday. Their flights were less than two hours from start to finish, but mine was over six. I arrived at midnight local time (2:00 A.M., New Orleans time). That translated to me being fucking exhausted. So, I grabbed a Red Bull and caught a cab to The Spa Atlantic Casino, checked in and texted them as to their whereabouts.

The three of us were tight in college and have done a stellar job of staying in touch, even though we no longer lived by one another. Technically, Joe and I were in college together. Nate had graduated at least five years prior, but had decided that his optimal career path was to pocket his MBA for a while and wait tables at Red Lobster, which is where Joe and I first met him. As the saying goes, "A good friend will bail you out of jail. But your best friends will be in jail next to you saying 'Damn! That was fun!'" These two would be the friends in jail next to me. They would also likely be the source of why I was there. Me?

Well, I'm normally the frontal lobe of our trio, doing my best to keep us all out of jail and reminding them that it might be a good idea to sleep just a little.

Anyway, they were at a bar named Jox. Normal people would go to the bar at the Casino, or head downtown to the hottest strip bars but not my friends. These idiots headed straight for the dive bar, like they were Reno natives.

I arrived at Jox with nothing more than a teeth-grinding buzz from the Red Bull and a bit of concern because these two had been at it since three in the afternoon.

Nate spotted me and yelled out to the bartender "Stu! This is Mike! Mike needs a Purple Nurple. Make it a double!"

At least seven Purple Nurples later, Stu tells us it's last call, but he adds that there's another bar called Doc Holliday Saloon where the local casino help like to party after hours. He then takes the liberty of calling us a cab.

Ten minutes later we piled in, Stu included.

I was drunk, but not like Nate, he was mono-syllabic at best and even then every word out of his mouth sounded like they had lost all their consonants; they were caveman-like grunts. I suggested, okay, I implied that maybe we ought to call it a night. Instead, we stuck to the plan. Doc Holliday's it was. We propped Nate on a barstool and got him comfy and then bee-lined for the pool table.

"I don't like you."

Someone was breathing down my neck. Nate couldn't have made it over to us that fast. Plus that voice sounded too low and way too sober to be his.

"I don't like you." The voice got louder. The voice was really enunciating. That definitely wasn't Nate.

I turned to find a guy glaring at me, or through me. I smirked, "Him or me?" I said as I pointed to Joe.

"You, fucker!" he growled.

Fuck. We had just gotten there. We barely had gotten our drinks. We hadn't talked to any of their women. What the hell? This sobered me up instinctually and I assessed. His long brown hair covered his ears which was what I wanted to see. A lot of MMA fighters live in Nevada. I wanted to see his ears. He could be one of them. My mind was reporting back other physical attributes:

-He's 180 lbs.

-6'1"

-I can't see his ears

-His nose has never been broken

-There's a beer bottle is in his right hand

-His jacket is on

-He's drunk but not incoherent

-I'm drunk, verging on incoherent…not so much anymore

"Let me see your ears." I requested.

"What the fuck do you want to see my ears for, faggot?" he retorted.

"Nothing, never mind." I replied.

Joe chuckled. I moved away. My inner list updated: not a fighter but watch the bottle.

An acquaintance of the angry patron whispered into his ear while escorting him back to his bar stool. Reluctantly, he complied, but not without first shoving the man hard while barking the battle cry of the drunken asshole, "Get the fuck off me, Bro!"

I wasn't looking for a fight and was glad that the intruder was now the asshole's focal point. I returned to Nate who—in his vowel-only caveman language—was convincing two ladies to go to a titty bar with us. Apparently the night was young, but I was still on New Orleans time. It was 4 A.M. in my brain. Nate started some chant about going to the titty bar. The ladies he was talking to chimed in.

"If you can't beat 'em!" I chimed in. Next thing I knew the six foot tall untrained local with the jacket and the beer bottle in his right hand was beside me.

"You going to the titty bar with us? You got money to go to the titty bar? If so, we're going. You wanna go? " It seemed like an appropriate and polite line of questioning.

"Fuck you, butthole!" he murmured as he squared up to me.

His body language stiffened, his eyes went narrow and he came in close, like men do when they're itching to fight.

The word butthole bothered me. It bothered me a lot. He could have called me asshole, faggot, fucker, anything. But for some reason butthole created a trigger in me. I think it's because if you call me an asshole or a fucker, well, those are names people use all the time. Butthole. Butthole? That conjured up all kinds of mental imagery, mainly of a couple of butt cheeks close to my face with the sphincter dead center staring me down. And that felt pretty damned offensive.

At that moment, if you would have put us side-by-side and

announced to the bar we were going to fight, eighty percent of the bar would have put a twenty spot on that guy. He looked that pissed. Also, I'm still all yuppie, so there's that.

Still not feeling like being in a fight but highly offended my response was "Ah, don't call me butthole."

It was a stupid response. There was no way that this guy was going to offer up an apology for the offense. I was now fully committed to the dance of the tards; the ritual where guys bark at each other to see if there is any bite.

"Fuck you, butthole," he retorted again slowly and deliberately.

The beer bottle in his right hand had rotated. It was now a weapon. He was going to hit me with it.

As he raised his hand my response came to me quick and without thought. Everything was slow in my mind. My left hand did a straight across grab onto his lapel; simultaneously my right hand reached over his shoulder and grabbed a handful of jacket. As I pulled him forward, my left foot pivoted to offset my balance and my right leg shot through the gap in between his legs.

The move is known in judo and jiu-jitsu circles as an uchi mata. This was the move I failed to pull off in the Worlds several years earlier. It must have been haunting me.

His height in the air shocked me. He should've gotten some frequent flyer miles for that ride. It shocked him too. The need to brace for his fall overrode the need for the beer bottle and his hand involuntarily released it and started flailing in the hopes of grabbing onto anything, anything to cushion the impact from the inevitable meeting with the floor. The beer bottle went even higher than he did.

He was so high in the air that I adjusted as we came crashing to the ground, easing his impact into the floor. In part it was a natural reaction from all the years of protecting training partners, but it was also because in all my years I had never so extremely tossed a person. I was so used to performing against trained and resistant partners that this throw on the untrained was extreme. It was too easy.

As the floor neared, he pulled a rookie bully move on me, a headlock. But, again, without thought I had already adjusted in anticipation of it, and I landed on top of him, in side control. His beer bottle fell from the sky onto my back rolling harmlessly onto the floor. I framed on his face, breaking his hands free of my neck. It was at that moment that I could sense the fight fleeing from his mind—*the mind is weak, the body is strong*—and the panic replacing his unsubstantiated anger. As I improved my position and took full side control with his right arm locked under my left, my mind had already identified attacks that would finish him: two variations of arm bars, arm control with a punch to jaw, mount to kimura, mount to ground and pound, and mount to a straight collar choke. And all of these attacks had entered my head at a speed that was instantaneous. From initiation to total control took maybe three seconds in real time, even though the event felt like it was in slow motion to me.

All my actions were mechanical and without thought, without anger, without malice. I was about to get nailed in the face with a beer bottle, and I reacted. And even with the elevation in Reno, my heart rate didn't feel like it was over eighty beats per minute. All the years of training, all of the repetition with resistant partners, this guy was not in my league. He was a sheep. He was the neophyte white belt walking through the door at the gym for the very first time.

As the attack options had me moving from side control to mount and a choke to finish, my frontal lobe interceded. *If you stop now, you probably won't get arrested.*

I paused and then I got in his face and said, "You are lucky. This could have gone so much worse for you." Pressing both collars with my full weight in his chest, I elevated myself to my feet, then pulled him to his feet, stayed in his face said, "Get the fuck away from me."

He was done. He knew he was the sheep. And, now I knew that I was more of a sheepdog than a wolf. I didn't have the kill in me.

The bartender tossed him. As I was wiping the beer off my back he came up to me. I figured I was next, but he handed me a beer instead. So, I apologized, thanked him for the beer and pulled up a barstool.

Side note: It's generally never a good idea to stick around after a fight. There are stories of guys getting their asses kicked or even worse. Some make their way back with a gun. I should have left. I didn't leave. Fortunately, he didn't come back.

Joe and Nate looked at me puzzled. Joe laced into me, "What the fuck are you doing, Mike!? Nate and I get us thrown out of bars. Your job is to stop us from getting thrown in jail." Then Joe took a step back and added, "I thought jiu-jitsu was ground fighting. What the fuck was that?!"

"We have to get our opponents to the ground first, Dummy. That throw was an uchi mata." I said to answer his question.

I was in the conversation, and went on to describe the uchi mata and to talk about the Worlds when I had blown that move, and my drunken partners were all ears. But in reality, I was pondering how surprised I was by the power I possessed. I felt like Peter Parker contemplating the spider web that just shot out of his wrist for the first time.

The night continued back at the casino. Joe and I played craps until the sun rose and we decided that it was time to get some sleep. Nate was MIA until noon the next day.

On Super Bowl Sunday, I said my goodbyes and grabbed a cab back to the airport. The Reno airport was a ghost town. There were six TSA agents to check my one carry-on bag. I made my way down the long empty hallways to my gate. You didn't think we had gotten together to actually watch the game, did you?

I sat on one of the chairs in a string of empty rows in the Reno terminal, the sun beaming in through the windows, warming the space in stark contrast to the chilled winter air outside as I contemplated the fight. Why was I surprised by the result? I had watched Royce Gracie dismantle larger opponents with jiu-jitsu in the early UFCs, and I had spent years dismantling brand new tough guy students like The Hell's Angels, the high school and college wrestlers, Aaron's brothers and the like. I know I didn't just save the planet or anything. This was just an asshole in a bar. But that was my first real fight since college. It was spontaneous. It was honest. And jiu-jitsu got me through it. I might be sitting here with my head bandaged, or minus an eye, or sitting in jail, if not for jiu-jitsu—the sport that I love. That sport is my religion, my therapist, my confidence, my salvation and I love jiu-jitsu. It has saved me from myself time and time again.

When I had first began practicing and could not catch my breath, Megaton told me, "There is the energy that you use when you train and practice. There is the energy that you use in a tournament. There is the energy that you use in an MMA fight and then there is the energy you use in a street fight." Based on what he said and the order he put them, I always assumed that the energy in the street fight would take the most energy, but it was the least. Also, there were always people who told me that jiu-jitsu doesn't work on the street. And, in the back of my mind, there was a tinge of doubt about the effectiveness of jiu-jitsu—or at least my jiu-jitsu—in a fight.

I called Sarah, I don't know why, out of habit I guess. She seemed to understand my need to train and fight. Maybe me fighting my way out of Crazyland helped her get out, too. I think out of everyone in the world, she knows me the best. As I told her the tale and explained how I was a bit surprised by my abilities, she merely said, "Of course you did that. You've been training for eight years, Mike. You're practically a Jedi."

A Jedi? That was the nicest thing she had ever said to me. I hung up and exhaled big. A small grin formed on my face. I looked down at the phone in my hand, not just because I probably looked like a big dork smiling at nothing and no one in the airport, but because, I don't know, maybe I thought the phone would smile back. Maybe I was hoping she was still holding her phone and smiling for no reason, too.

Come to think of it, my ex had said plenty of nice things to me in our twelve years of marriage. The warmth of the sun coming through the wall of windows relaxed me. My mind was at peace as it strayed from jiu-jitsu and started to think of some of the nice things she said.

Epilogue

Several years ago, I sat with my old college buddy Joe on his beach house patio, watching the sunset, listening to Buffet (what a cliché, I know) and drinking cervesas. He's my most successful friend who, like me, began in modest beginnings. I am always curious as to what makes people tick, so I asked him about his career success. He told me a story from his freshman year in college. His fraternity volunteered to clean up Sun Devil Stadium after a game. As Joe looked around at all the vacant seats in the stadium, he thought about how each one of those seats could represent a day of his life. And when that day was over, he would move to the next seat, never to return to the seat he just left.

It was at that point in the story where the engineer in me interjected and pointed out that Sun Devil Stadium has 72,000 seats, which meant he was planning on living to the better part of two hundred years. He responded with something to the effect of, "Do you want to crap on my point or listen to what I'm saying?" I shut up. Joe continued. Once he had put his mortality into perspective - coupled with the fact that twenty years worth of stadium seats were already gone - he swore to live each day to its fullest and not to be impeded by doubt.

I thought about Joe's parable. Then I engineered it some more and recognized that by the time you take out sleeping, eating, school, work and commuting from the more realistic "30,000 seat stadium," you are only left with about 9,000 seats for yourself and your passions. 9,000 seats?! Sometimes it doesn't pay to think like an engineer. Seventy two thousand seats to play with was a nice big number. There's plenty of room for error with 72,000 seats to use up in a lifetime. But with only 9,000 seats realistically, well, those could waste away before your very eyes if you didn't watch yourself and mind your time. And Joe's analogy coincided with something that another friend, Aaron had told me once. He said after you account for sleep, work and family there's room for only one or maybe two other pursuits, and that's it.

I have used close to one thousand of those seats spending my afternoons in a dojo, following a passion known as jiu-jitsu. And every one of those seats has been on the fifty-yard line.

And I have no regrets.

Glossary of Techniques

Arm Bar
Chapters: 3, 13, 16, 19, 22, 34, 41
© 2013 Michael R. Simpson

Arm Triangle
Chapter 38
© 2013 Michael R. Simpson

Darce Choke
Chapter 36
© 2013 Michael R. Simpson

Flower Sweep
Chapters: 19, 38
© 2013 Michael R. Simpson

Guard

Chapters: 3, 5, 6, 11, 12, 14, 15, 16, 19, 22, 24, 34, 35, 36, 38, 39

© 2013 Michael R. Simpson

Half Guard

Chapters: 12, 22, 38

© 2013 Michael R. Simpson

Mount
Chapters 12, 14, 16, 19, 21, 22, 34, 41
© 2013 Michael R. Simpson

Omaplata
Chapter 34
© 2013 Michael R. Simpson

Rear Naked Choke
Chapters: 4, 10, 16, 22, 33, 38, 40
© 2013 Michael R. Simpson

Side Control
Chapters: 11, 16, 19, 22, 34, 41
© 2013 Michael R. Simpson

Bibliography

1 Herman, Villa and Whiting, 'Batman Stops Crash Suspect; Arizona' Arizona Republic 22 March 2002. www.freerepublic.com/focus/f-news/651585/posts [Accessed 11/5/2012]

2 Uploaded by CaughtOnTape TV 'High Speed Dump Truck Chase and Flip', 14 April 2010, http://www.youtube.com/watch?v=LGPgxfB87Cs [Accessed 12/11/2012]

3 Pela, Robert L., 'He's Bat Man' Phoenix New Times 20 June 2002. www.phoenixnewtimes.com/2002-06-20/culture/he-s-nat-man/ [Accessed 11/5/2012]

4 Maricopa County Superior Court Website, http://www.superiorcourt.maricopa.gov/docket/CriminalCourt Cases/caseInfo/ [Accessed 11/5/2012]

5 Sherdog Website, www.sherdog.com/fighter/Doug-Click-7242 [Accessed 12/11/2012]

6 International Brazilian Jiu-jitsu Federation Website, www.ibjjf.org/results/1998panamericano.htm [Accessed 12/11/2012]

7 Agar, John, 'Iraq War Veteran, Mixed-Martial Arts Fighter Recalls Halting Grand Rapids Robbery (Video)' http://www.mlive.com/news/grand-rapids/index.ssf/2012/03/iraq_war_veteran_mixed-martial.html [Accessed 12/3/2012]

8 Balboa, Lixzzy, 'Student Vet Thwarts GR Robbery', 26 March 2012, http://www.lanthorn.com/index.php/article/2012/03/student_vet_thwarts_gr_robbery. [Accessed 12/11/2012]

9 Ibid

10 Video Fox News. www.video.foxnews.com/v/1541069779001/vet-uses-mma-move-to-stop-robbery, 1, April 2012 [Accessed 11/5/2012]

11 Gracie, Roger, 'Guest Editor' Jiu-jitsu Style Magazine, Sept/Oct 2012 Edition.

12 IMBD Website, http://www.imdb.com/name/nm2599210/bio [Accessed 12/13/2012]

13 Hartman, Barry, Fight Corner Online 'McSweeney's Robbery Twarting Paints MMA Fighters in a Positive Light' 24 August 2012 http://www.mmafightcorner.com/2012/08/26/james-mcsweeneys-robbery-thwarting-paints-mma-fighters-positive-light/ [Accessed 12/3/2012]

14 Cavalleri, Gaston Blog 'The New York Post - A mugging in New York's Central Park goes bad.' 9 July 2012 http://gastoncavalleri.com/2012/07/09/a-stroll-in-the-park-3/ [Accessed 12/27/2012]

15 Sanderson, Bill 'The New York Post - A mugging in New York's Central Park goes bad.' 9 July 2012 http://gastoncavalleri.com/2012/07/09/a-stroll-in-the-park-3/ [Accessed 12/27/2012]

16 "Jon Jones Stops Mugger Hours Before UFC 128"March 9 2012 http://www.fightertrends.com/mma-news/ufc/jon-jones-stops-mugger-hours-before-ufc-128/ [Accessed 1/5/2013]

17 UFC 128 Jon Jones Talks About the Mugger Youtube Video. http://www.youtube.com/watch?v=L9qFlAoRym0 3/20/2011- [Accessed 1/5/2013]

18 Gladwell, Malcom "Outliers" November 18, 2008

19 Robert Scaglione, William Cummins, Karate of Okinawa: Building Warrior Spirit, Tuttle Publishing, 1993,   (this source was Wikipedia and was the source cited in Wiki)

20 http://www.jarrodbunch.com/bio.html [Accessed 1/10/13]

21 Stefano Esposito and Tina Sfondeles, 'Mugger Picks Wrong Victim: MMA Fighter' Chicago Sun Times; 5 December 2011. [http://www.suntimes.com/news/crime/9261611-418/mugger-chooses-wrong-victim-ultimate-fighting-champ.html [Accessed 1/15/2011]

22 Aldex, Mike, 'Jiu-jitsu instructor saves San Francisco police officer from attack' San Francisco Examiner; 17 April 2011. http://www.sfexaminer.com/local/2011/04/jiu-jitsu-instructor-saves-officer-during-pummeling#ixzz2IzOfcXCo [Accessed 1/24/2013]

23 Caleb (host), "Pod Cast 240 - Interview with Pedro Arrigoni" The Fight Works

Podcast; 24 April 2011. [Accessed 1/24/2013]

24 Staff Report, 'VIDOE: Jiu-jitsu instructor saves San Francisco police officer from attack' San Francisco Examiner; 20 April 2011.
http://www.sfexaminer.com/local/crime/2011/04/video-jiu-jitsu-instructor-saving-san-francisco-police-officer-attack
[Accessed 1/24/2013]

25 Lohr, David, 'Man in Wheelchair Thwarts Attempted Robbery' AOL News; 10 November 2010. http://www.aolnews.com/2010/11/10/man-in-wheelchair-thwarts-attempted-robbery/
[Accessed 2/6/2013]

26 Iole, Kevin, 'UFC's Nick King rushes to rescue couple being mugged in Calgary' Cagewriter; 7 June 2012. http://sports.yahoo.com/blogs/mma-cagewriter/ufc-nick-ring-rushes-rescue-couple-being-mugged-211812532.html [Accessed 2/13/2013]

27 Marrocco, Steven, 'MMA legend Renzo Gracie live tweets attempted mugging, gives perps raccoon eyes' Cagewriter; 7 September 2012.
http://www.mmajunkie.com/news/2012/09/mma-legend-renzo-gracie-live-tweets-attempted-mugging-gives-perps-raccoon-eyes
[Accessed 3/8/2013]

28 MMA 'Renzo Gracie reports mugging real time over Twitter' GracieMag; 7 September 2012. http://www.graciemag.com/2012/09/renzo-makes-history-and-reports-mugging-real-time-over-twitter/
[Accessed 3/8/2013]

29 Ayres, Ian and Levitt, Steven 'MMA 'Measuring Positive Externalities from Unobservable Victim Precaution: An Empirical Analysis of Lojack' The Quarterly Journal of Economics Vol 113 No 1 (Feb 1998) 43-77 [http://pricetheory.uchica-go.edu/levitt/Papers/LevittAyres1998.pdf]

30 McCann, Jaymi 'US sailor thwarts Dubai bus driver rapist after putting him in strangehold with her thighs and then beating him into submission ' 25 April 2013; http://www.dailymail.co.uk/news/article-2314631/US-sailor-thwarts-Dubai-bus-driver-rapist-putting-strangehold-thighs-beating-submission.html
[Accessed 6/25/2013]

31 Habiba Ahmed Abd Elaziz 'Female sailor escapes rape during Dubai visit' 25

April 2013; http://www.dailymail.co.uk/news/article-2314631/US-sailor-thwarts-Dubai-bus-driver-rapist-putting-strangehold-thighs-beating-submission.html [Accessed 6/25/2013]

32 Wilson, Kimberly 'Eugene mixed martial artist describes foiling armed robbery at Los Angeles motel' 7 November 2011; http://www.oregonlive.com/pacific-north-west-news/index.ssf/2011/11/eugene_mixed_martial_artist_de.html [Accessed 3/12/2013]

33 Hotel Robber Nabbed by Good Samaritans Visiting Los Angeles for Martial Arts Tournament Youtube Video. http://www.youtube.com/watch?v=QUntJ2Js3T8&feature=youtu.be [Accessed 3/12/2013]